The Adventures of
PEE & POO

The Fun Potty Training Book

BY DAFNE NICOU ENGSTROM WITH ELSA & LUCA

THE ADVENTURES OF PEE AND POO
The *Fun* Potty Training Story Book

By Dafne Nicou Engstrom with Elsa & Luca

Published by: StardustBooks.net

ISBN: 978-0692527450

Design: Let's Write Books, Inc.

Illustration: Vladimir Milosavljevic

A Note to Parents from Phyllis Cath, MD

Even in our modern child-centered culture, we as parents are often challenged to talk with our very young children in a manner that actually reflects how they perceive the world.

In my almost forty years of practicing child psychiatry, I have found that parents often ask, "How can we talk with our toddlers? What will they understand? How can we learn what is on their minds?" I often answer, "Play with them, read to them, and listen to their reactions. They will tell you what is on their minds and what is troubling them. They will guide you."

Young children are fabulous communicators but in their own way. They don't respond well to direct questions, but they will tell you the most intimate things through storytelling or in their play.

Although the title of this book might seem shocking to some adults, the author actually speaks to how young children think. Young children experience the world more directly through their bodies and senses. This book is a show and tell, it will open conversations.

Toddlers who are potty or toilet training are attempting to regulate their bodily functions. From the toddlers' point of view, suddenly adults are asking them to be more self-reliant and independent. The requests and the developmental skills that are required of them often leave children worried and afraid. They wonder, "Where does my pee and poo go? What happens to my pee and poo? What happens to me if I give up my pee and poo to the toilet? Could other parts of me also be flushed down? And, what happens if I give up the safety of being a baby and do all these very important things on my own? Am I capable of that?"

At the same age as potty training is taking place, children normally will start other activities, like being a part of a play group. The person that usually accompanies them might leave, and the little ones are left to fend for themselves for the first time in a new environment. During this sensitive stage of development, parents can often observe fears and increased separation anxiety, accentuated worries about minor body injuries, nightmares, and even phobias.

For example, Max, a 3 ½-year-old tense boy was unable to toilet train. He revealed to me that he was worried about losing body parts down the toilet. Once reassured that the feared event would not happen, he decided that God must have provided a special glue to keep little boys from losing their precious parts. At last, he was able to begin his toilet training.

You may also be surprised to find that 4 to 5-year-old children might enjoy this book as well. These young, already potty-trained children will remember the struggle they had to gain these important skills. They will enthusiastically and gleefully talk about pee and poo as they giggle and enjoy feeling safe in their newly acquired superior abilities.

Sometimes though, already potty-trained young children who are under stress, may regress and start wetting their pants again. In such cases, it can be very helpful to read this book to them and have conversations about pee and poo. Young children need to know that going to the bathroom is natural, that it is not dangerous, and is nothing to be ashamed of.

The Adventures of Pee and Poo will help your child master one of life's most important early achievements. Through playful characters, pictures, and words, you will be able to join your children's world and help them feel comfortable with toilet training and learning to understand their body's natural processes.

Phyllis Cath, MD
Associate Clinical Professor
Department of Psychiatry
University of California, San Francisco

4

Little Karen was in a terrible mood.

Her mother did not allow her to go to the park to play with her best friend. It was getting late and her mother was busy with cleaning up after dinner.

"You are so mean!" she screamed as she ran to her bathroom and locked the door behind her.

"I'm not going to brush my teeth, and I don't want to put on my pajamas," she hissed.

"Sweetheart, aren't you going to say goodnight to us?" asked her mother through the locked bathroom door. "No, I am not!" answered Karen. "You are not nice to me!"

Then Karen sat down and used her potty, but she did not empty it. "Someone else can do that!" she whispered between her teeth as she ran to her room and crawled into bed. "Nobody likes me," she sobbed.

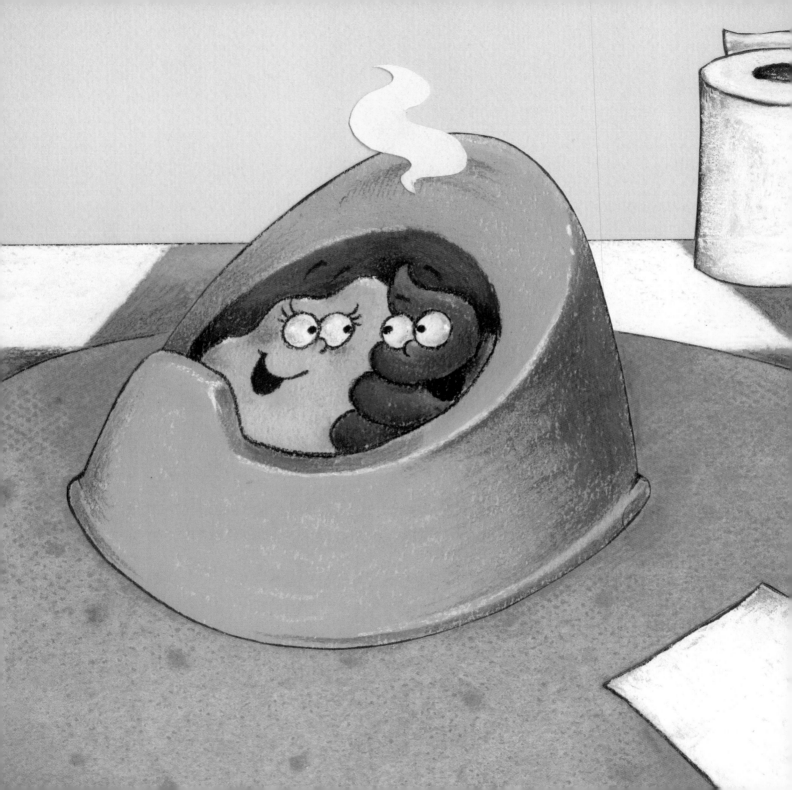

In the quiet bathroom, the newly born Pee and Poo lay motionless in the potty.

"She didn't flush us down?" whispered Pee.

"I know," answered Poo, "and maybe the parents don't know we are here. I just heard them pass the bathroom door! This could be a great chance for us to escape!"

"How are we going to get out of here?" whispered Pee. "If I leave the potty, I will sink into the bathroom rug, and that will be the end of me!"

9

"I have an idea," said Poo quietly.

"Why don't I pour you into an empty bottle? I see one sitting on the edge of the sink right above us. I'll try to get up there and push it down!"

"Brilliant!" said Pee.

Poo managed to climb up to the edge of the potty where he could see the bathroom floor. "There is a loose piece of toilet paper sitting below me," he said. "If I jump, I'll land right on the paper. I could use it as slippers and not make a mess on the bathroom floor!"

"Try it!" whispered Pee.

"Yohoo!" shouted Poo as he plunged to the floor and landed right on the toilet paper.

11

Poor Pee could see nothing inside the potty, but she could hear Poo grunting as he was climbing up to the sink toward the bottle.

Then she heard him call out, "I did it! I am by the sink now. Here comes the bottle!"

Pee heard a thud as it hit the floor. "Oh," she thought, all excited, "I will now have my own place to live in!"

Poo was very pleased with himself as he climbed down again to the bathroom floor. "That was easy," he said, "but now comes the tricky part. I'll have to put the empty bottle precisely under the spout of the potty, so when I start pouring you, I don't spill you."

Poo got the newfound bottle in place, and then he went behind the potty and tilted it. The spout was lowered over the open bottle. "Brace yourself, Pee," he said, "here we go!"

Pee was airborne, and a golden ray of her poured from the potty into the bottle. It was perfect. Not a drop of her spilled!

13

Poo quickly put a cork into the bottle.

Pee was now safe! Then he looked at himself and said, "I can't leave the bathroom like this. I have to put on some clothes!" He looked around, and he saw one of Karen's flowery handkerchiefs lying on the floor next to the dirty laundry basket. "This one is for me," he said quietly as he wrapped himself in the soft, flowery cloth.

"Oh my!" laughed Pee. "You look so cute in that dress!" "Don't tease me!" growled Poo. "Let's get moving!!"

15

He started rolling Pee's bottle in front of him, and they quietly left the bathroom. When they got into the living room, the bottle hit something on the floor. At the same time, they heard a noise from the other end of the room, and a blue Mercedes toy truck came roaring against them. Poo felt the truck brush by him, and then it ran into the wall and stopped.

"A remote control truck," whispered Poo.

"The bottle must have hit the remote! How exciting! We could use this truck to ride in!"

"Could we go and buy cupcakes?" asked Pee. "Yes," said Poo proudly. "It will be an honor for me to drive you!"

He lifted Pee onto the truck and with the remote in hand climbed into the driver's seat. With a big grin he said, "Now, the next thing is to get out of the house without being caught. I think we will wait by the front door till the father leaves the house in the morning."

Pee and Poo managed to get a few hours of sleep and woke when the father was making his morning coffee in the kitchen. After a while, they heard his steps coming towards them. Then the steps stopped. "It smells really bad here," he mumbled. "I'll have to check it out when I come home this evening."

As he opened the front door to leave, he remembered that he had left his cell phone on the kitchen table. He went back in again, and he did not close the door…

"Today is our lucky day!" exclaimed Poo.

He pressed the remote and, without being seen, out the open door they went!

"Wow, it's pretty outdoors!" said a smiling Pee.

"Now, where do we buy cupcakes?"

As they were driving along, people everywhere stopped and said, "Look! What is that? A bottle of lemonade and a hot dog in a flowery dress on a Mercedes toy truck! Cool! But what is that bad smell?"

Poo and Pee pretended not to hear them.

Finally, they saw a blue and yellow awning that read,

"GLUTEN-FREE CUPCAKES"

Poo quickly made a U-turn and drove right into the store.

"This will be fun!" said Pee as she rolled off the truck, and they went to stand in line in the busy store. Soon it was their turn, and Poo stepped up to the counter and held forth a five-dollar bill that he had just found on the floor.

"We would like to have two cupcakes, one vanilla and one mint," said Poo to the girl behind the counter. "Please put them here on the back of our truck." When the girl bent down to place the cupcakes on the truck she said, "You stink! Please get out of the store right away!"

23

Saddened, Poo drove the truck out onto the sidewalk.

He was so upset that he did not pay attention to the curb, and the truck went over the edge and into the gutter. Pee and Poo were thrown out and landed in the street.

Shook up, but not hurt, Pee finally said, "Why don't we eat our cupcakes before some street cleaning truck comes and sweeps us into its garbage hull?" "You are right," said Poo. "Come here, sweetheart. Let me uncork your bottle, so you can get to your cupcake."

Just as Pee had finished eating her mint-flavored treat, she heard a street cleaning truck coming their way. "Help!" she screamed.

"There must be someone that can help us!"

Scared, they both started crying.

When the street cleaning truck was only a block away, three dogs came walking by. "Hey you, why are you crying?" said one of them who was a poodle. "I wrecked our truck," sobbed Poo. "We are stuck in the gutter, and the street cleaning truck is coming. I smell bad, and people are laughing at me, and my friend Pee here cannot move so well because she lives in a bottle." Poo kept crying. He did not know what to do.

"I'm sure it can't be all that bad," said the kind poodle, "but let me see now if I understand. You are a Pee living in a bottle and a Poo wrapped in a flowery handkerchief, and you have just wrecked your truck. That is very unusual and also very interesting!"

"Very interesting!" said the other two dogs.

"Can you help us?" asked Poo. "I'm sure we can!" answered the poodle, wagging his tail. "Why don't you come with us to the park?"

"That would be wonderful," answered Pee and Poo, and they managed a shy smile.

"OK. Great! Let's go!" ordered the poodle, and the three dogs quickly put Pee and Poo into the truck and then lifted them back onto the sidewalk. Right when they were done, the street cleaning truck came and cleaned the gutter. Poo shuddered and little waves could be seen in the bottle as Pee's heart rate increased.

"Now, that was a close call," said the poodle, whose name was Charlie. "But nothing bad happened, so let's move on!" The truck is broken, but we can push you with our noses!"

Soon they arrived in the pretty park, and they stopped next to a flowering bush to rest.

"I have an idea," said Charlie. "You want to be beautiful and smell good, right?"

"Yes, yes," said Pee and Poo at the same time.

"You know," continued Charlie, "the best food for flowers is all types of pee and poo mixed with water. Looking at the sky, I think it is going to rain. Poo, you will soften when you get wet, and we can uncork your bottle, Pee, and let you flow into the grass. You could both join the rainwater and soak into the ground. What a feast for the flowers!!!!"

"Will it hurt?" wondered Poo.

"Absolutely not!" answered Charlie, and then he said, "Pretty soon, you will grow back as a part of some beautiful, fragrant flowers!"

"Are you serious?" asked Pee. "Cross my heart," said Charlie.

"Then, let's do it!" squealed Pee and Poo.

The three dogs gently poured Pee into the grass, and they put Poo next to her. They high fived each other, and Pee and Poo closed their eyes. Then it started to rain!

* * *

31

Three months later, little Karen and her mother were walking in the park. "Mamma, mamma," shouted Karen. "Look at the beautiful flowers over there by the big bush.

Let me pick some for you!!"

Quickly, she ran over to the fragrant flowers and picked a bouquet that she gave to her grateful mother.

"And mamma," she said, "look what I found under the bush behind the flowers!" She held out a neatly folded, flowery handkerchief and a blue remote control truck.

"They look just like the ones that disappeared some months ago!" said Karen's mother. "How strange!! But let's head home now. It's getting late!"

Just as they left the park, three playing dogs ran by with their tails high. It looked like they were waving "Hello!"

Sitting in a blue, beautiful vase in little Karen's home, the flowers looked at each other.

Their beautiful smiles were visible only to those who had stardust in their eyes…

THE END

About the Author

For Dafne Nicou Engstrom, storytelling has always been an important part of her life. With her multicultural, European family background, there has been plenty of inspiration.

Last year, while visiting her oldest daughter in New York, her grandson Luca asked her to tell him a story. She said, "OK, give me a word, and I will build a story around it." Luca looked at her, mischief in his eyes, and said, "Poo!"

The story was started, and Luca helped Dafne build it with his wonderful, quick wit and imagination. When they came to THE END, Luca looked at her and said, "Mormor (grandmother), you are a good storyteller."

A week later, Dafne was back in her hometown of San Francisco having dinner with her younger daughter and her family. At bedtime, Dafne was asked by her granddaughter Elsa to tell a story. Naturally, the Poo story was fresh in her mind, and Elsa quickly added more adventures to the plot — adventures created by an uninhibited, humoristic soul.

Through the inspiration and imagination of her grandchildren, "The Adventures of Pee and Poo" was born!

Look for additional children's books from Dafne Nicou Engstrom including *Teddy Went A-Walking, Nico and the Ice Cream Caper, and others!*

Visit her website to learn more: www.StardustBooks.net

Contact Dafne Nicou Engstrom at Dafne@StardustBooks.net

Thames & Hudson

THIS AIN'T NO DISCO

new wave album covers

By Jennifer McKnight-Trontz

For Esme, Ian, Deborah and James Patrick.

Thanks to the record labels, artists, designers, and photographers responsible for producing the wonderful album cover art featured in this collection. Thanks to the publishers, as always, it has been a pleasure. A special thanks to my editors, Alan Rapp and Leslie Davisson, and to Vivien Sung for her design direction. Thanks to all those who contributed their albums: Lisa Bach, Michael Beller, Mikyla Bruder, Leslie Davisson, Steve Moore, Randy Stratton, Alan Rapp, Michelle Soto, and Richard Reddig. Lastly, thanks to Gregg Brown for his photography of some of the albums.

First published in the United Kingdom in 2005 by Thames & Hudson Ltd,
181A High Holborn, London WC1V 7QX

www.thamesandhudson.com

First published in the United States of America in 2005 by Chronicle Books LLC.

© 2005 by Jennifer McKnight-Trontz

Book design by Jennifer McKnight-Trontz

The title, "This Ain't No Disco" from Talking Heads' "Life During Wartime" © 1979 Index Music/Bleu Disque Music Co., Inc. (ASCAP).

British Library Cataloguing-in-Publication Data
A catalogue record for this book is available from the British Library

ISBN–10:   0-500-28550-0

ISBN–13:   978-0-500-28550-3

Printed and bound in Hong Kong

CONTENTS

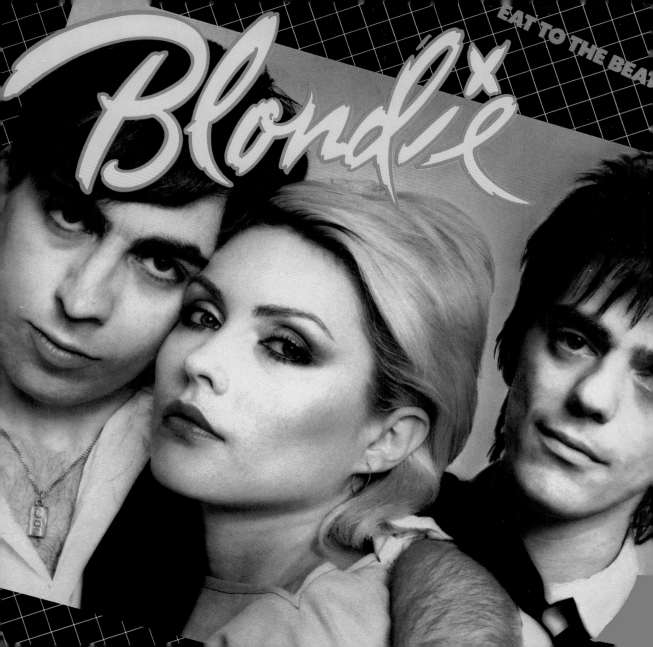

INTRODUCTION

And in the beginning, there was New Wave.

Well, not exactly. Punk had to happen first. But, sprouting out of the anarchic energy of the Sex Pistols and the working-class, three-chord glory of the Ramones came the spirited sounds of New Wave, with a similar liberated ethos, but in an entertaining and curious mix of art, fashion, and music. Both Punk and New Wave were a reaction to the slick, uninspired arena-rock and Top 40 pop bloating the air-waves of the 1970s. Like Punk, New Wave could be edgy and confrontational, but its advent called for a renewal of pure (albeit stylized) fun in music with less concern for the world's perceived injustices—if any were perceived at all. In keeping with Punk's spirit of rebellion and assaulting the status quo, New Wave stirred things up by stirring things together.

New Wave consisted of artists as divergent as Elvis Costello and Joy Division, Stray Cats and Naked Eyes, and Siouxsie and the Banshees and Katrina and the Waves. New Wave comprised Post-Punk, Synth-Pop, Neo-Psychedelia, Neo-Mod, Power Pop, New Romantic, 2-Tone, Art-Rock, Rockabilly, and Goth—styles that at first blush didn't fit the Top 40 sounds on the radio. Soon enough, natu-rally, songs in all these subgenres climbed their way to the top of the charts. What unified New Wave artists, as Ira Robbins explained in his 1983 compendium *The Trouser Press Guide to New Wave Records*, is "a sense that rock music should be explored, enjoyed, attacked, converted—anything but simply exploited."

A spirit of outrageousness and novelty permeated New Wave—especially an appreciation of the synthetic and artificial. Bands like Devo built a world of nylon and plastic in their visual identity and album covers. There were the B-52's and their mile-high beehives,

Eat to the Beat
BLONDIE
Cover art: Norman Seeff/
John Van Hamersveld/Billy Bass
Chrysalis, 1979

and bands with names like the Silicon Teens. As performers, New Wave artists drew upon this vocabulary of images and ideas; at the same time, as musicians, they embraced the new electronic sounds of synthesizers, sequencers, and drum machines. And the covers followed, both flamboyant and cautionary, such as those that glorified the technological advances in society while acknowledging their dangers: Mi-Sex's *Computer Games* features a male and female mannequin stamped with bar codes. Yellow Magic Orchestra's first album features a geisha with her head exploding in wires.

The album covers reflected the drama and novelty of the music inside. While Punk album cover graphics were defiant, of the torn-paper and blackmail-lettering sort, New Wave covers were more innovative, stylized, and sophisticated, often with an element of futurism. Comparing Punk and New Wave, legendary album designer Roger Dean wrote in his 1982 book *The Album Cover Album* (2nd volume), "the sleeve style changed along with the clothes and image presentation. [New Wave covers featured] unashamed cobbling together of old '50s styles, bright garish colors, lines and bars from the '30s and the quasi-technical graphics of the computer age." But unlike the first generation of Punk output, the albums were "designed, and thought out to a degree."

Designers often found inspiration from previous art movements, such as Dada, Futurism, Constructivism, De Stijl, and Bauhaus.

Album cover designer Nick de Ville explained New Wave's style in *Album: Style and Image in Sleeve Design*: "Following punk's pillage of the Situationist lexicon, there was a reaching out for other

Look Sharp!
JOE JACKSON
Cover art: Michael Ross
Photography: Brian Griffin
A&M, 1979

graphic forms with revolutionary credentials . . . [including] Russian constructivist tropes—bold, simple forms (including cut-out photographic elements), a restricted range of primary colours, emphatic sans-serif typefaces and liberal use of diagonals underpinning the dynamism of the layout."

As it was sometimes hard to make out what the emergent, multi-styled music genre was, expectations were hard to confound. Still, through the album covers, a visual frame emerged, and boundaries were pushed. For example, Bow Wow Wow's cover for *See Jungle! See Jungle!* is a re-creation of Edouard Manet's controversial 1863 painting *Le Dejeuner sur l'Herbe*, with the band's fourteen-year-old singer, Annabella Lwin, appearing naked. There's a masked and aggressively androgynous Annie Lenox with close-cropped, flame-red hair on *Touch*; Gary Numan's unsettling robotic appearance on *Replicas*; Joe Jackson's isolated white shoes on *Look Sharp!* Peter Saville's cover for New Order's *Power Corruption and Lies* manages to gracefully combine high-tech graphics with Henri Fantin-Latour's nineteenth-century painting *Roses*. The back cover, modeled after a floppy disk, represents the band's exploration of computer-generated music.

Like the album designers, some New Wave bands looked to the past for their inspiration, resurrecting 1960s Mod, Jamaican Ska, and 1950s Rockabilly. New Wave was the first music genre to so thoroughly revisit past genres. These covers, especially, used vintage graphics, typography, and fashion to tap into the style codes of the music's era. The Rockabilly revival group Stray Cats sported '50s-inspired sideburns, pompadours, and leather jackets. The cover of *Rant n' Rave* features the band as greaser mechanics. Soon after the debut of the Jam's *In the City*, fans were copying the band's peg-pant suits, buttoned shirts, and short, neat hairstyles. The New Romantics, who owed much of their style sense to the Elizabethan and Victorian looks of 1970s artists like Roxy Music and David Bowie, succeeded in making frilly shirts, velvet, and make-up look "good" on men in an unthreatening way. The covers for New Ro bands like Duran Duran and Adam and the Ants were as much about the flamboyant dress and image of the group as the album's design. A glossy portrait of the artist or band was a slick way to market the music, especially as the artists themselves became more popular and more identified with a signature look. The work of "art" on the cover of *Prince Charming* is Adam Ant himself, done up in ruffles, bright lipstick, heavy eye makeup, and fingernail polish.

In concert with the do-it-yourself attitude of the musicians and the influence of small independent labels, the New Wave movement succeeded in artfully combining creative disciplines. This was a significant era in which the music, style, and graphic design all worked together to emphasize the newness of the genre. There were musicians who were designers, designers (both graphic and fashion) who influenced musicians, and designers and musicians who ran record labels. Bryan Ferry had a hand in the design of many Roxy Music covers, including the controversial *Country Life*, featuring two panty-clad models. Bauhaus, Squeeze, and Adam Ant also contributed to their covers. Graphic designer Peter Saville was a founder of Manchester's Factory Records. Three of the Talking Heads' members met at the Rhode Island School of Design. The band's lead,

Touch
EURYTHMICS
Cover art: Laurence Stevens
Photography: Peter Ashworth
RCA, 1983

David Byrne, contributed to the cover design of their second album, *More About Buildings and Food*, as did keyboardist/guitarist Jerry Harrison on their third, *Fear of Music*. The embossed black cardboard cover was nominated for an album design Grammy in 1979. Devo played a significant role in the design of their covers and in the marketing of their music and paraphernalia. The band's "Club Devo" sold 3-D Glasses, leisure suits, and spud rings. The band took a cut in royalties in order to have perforation on the cover of *Duty Now for the Future.*

New Wave kept music, fashion, and design fun and forward-looking, and most important, in conversation with one another. This was the last significant genre of music before the death of the LP, and therefore the last to exploit the glorious potential of the 12" square canvas. New Wave was the bridge into the MTV generation, with the Buggles ushering the video age with the very first video played on the network: *Video Killed the Radio Star*. Without New Wave, Patrick Nagel's artwork wouldn't have inspired the style of legions of mall-going teens, no one would know why Frankie went to Hollywood, how to "Choose Life" or "Whip it good." The legacy of New Wave continues, with music lovers collecting New Wave albums, current fashions incorporating the graphics and vibrant color palettes of the time, and the sounds of contemporary bands paying tribute to the artists. The more than 300 album covers on these pages are a portrait of an era, and a testament to the great energy of New Wave.

12

See Jungle! See Jungle!
BOW WOW WOW
Cover art: Nick Egan
Photography: Andy Earl
RCA, 1981

Three musicians from Adam and the Ants—Matthew Ashman, Leroy Gorman, and Dave Barberossa—left to join Malcolm McLaren's creation Bow Wow Wow. This cover caused a sensation when it was discovered that the band's lead singer, Annabella Lwin, was only fourteen.

violent femmes

VIOLENT FEMMES
Cover art: Jeff Price
Photography: Ron Hugo
Slash/Warner Bros., 1983

14

Business As Usual
MEN AT WORK
Cover art: John Dickson
Columbia, 1982

15

The Crossing
BIG COUNTRY
Cover art: J.B.&Q Branch
Mercury, 1983

CULTURE CLUB

kissing to be clever

16

Kissing to Be Clever
CULTURE CLUB
Cover art: Jfk Graham
Virgin/Epic, 1982

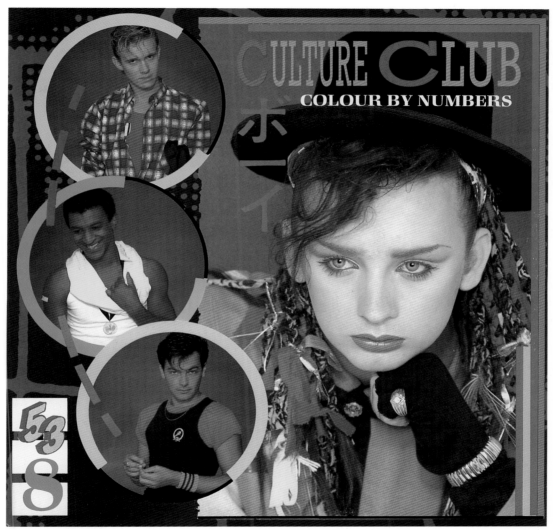

Like many Assorted Images covers, Colour by Numbers *combines various typographic elements and geometric shapes.*

Colour by Numbers
CULTURE CLUB
Cover art: Assorted Images
Photography: Jamie Morgan
Virgin, 1983

ST-12228

MISSING
PERSONS

SPRING SESSiON M

18

Spring Session M
MISSING PERSONS
Cover art: Glen Wexler/Kurt Triffet
Capitol, 1982

19

Pleasure Victim
BERLIN
Cover art: Mark Ulves/Cadillac Graphics
Enigma/Geffen, 1982

Trans-Europe Express
KRAFTWERK
Cover art: J. Stara
Capitol, 1976

The Man-Machine
KRAFTWERK
Cover art: Florian Schneider/Karl Klefisch
Photography: Gunter Frohling
Capitol, 1978

Autobahn
KRAFTWERK
Cover art: Emil Schult
Vertigo/Phonogram, 1974

In 1974 Kraftwerk (German for "power station") released Autobahn. *The hit title-track simulated a twenty-minute car drive accompanied by synthesizers and sound effects.* The Man-Machine *was inspired by the art of El Lissitzky, a Russian painter and propagandist for the Stalinist regime.*

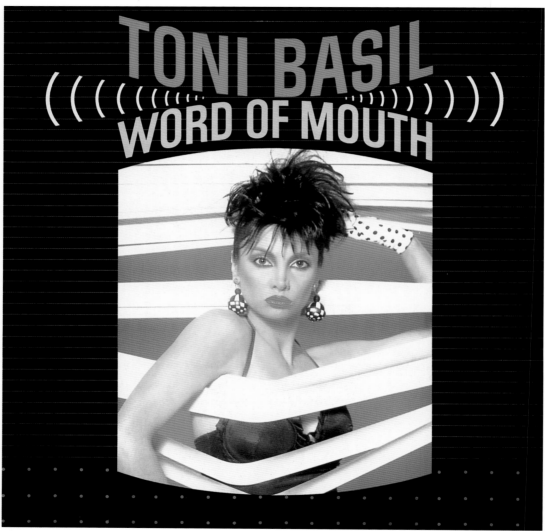

Word of Mouth
TONI BASIL
Cover art: Janet Levinson
Photography: Steven Arnold
Radialchoice/Chrysalis, 1981

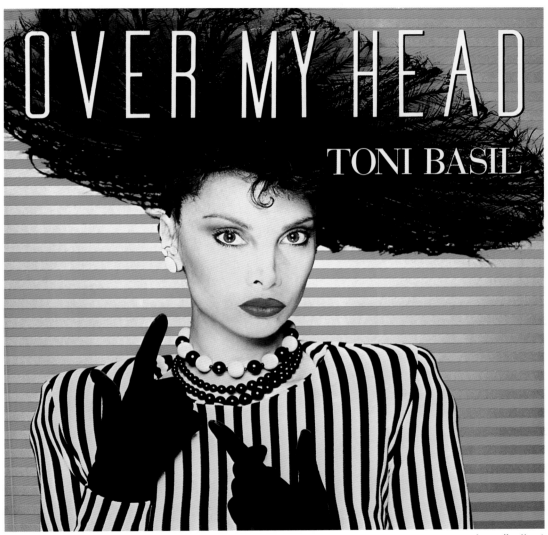

OVER MY HEAD

TONI BASIL

Over My Head
TONI BASIL
Cover art: Richard Seireeni/Jerry Casale
Photography: Allen Ballard
Radialchoice/Chrysalis, 1983

ACTUAL SIZE

R.BARGE

Q: Are We Not Men?

DEVO

Uncontrollable Urge • (I Can't Get No)
Satisfaction • Praying Hands •
Space Junk • Mongoloid • Jocko Homo •
Too Much Paranoia • Gut Feeling/(Slap
Your Mammy) • Come Back Jonee •
Sloppy (I Saw My Baby Gettin') •
Shrivel-Up

Q: Are We Not Men? A: We are Devo!
DEVO
Cover art: John Cabalka/Devo/Erik Munson
Warner Bros., 1978

Devo covers often featured images culled from '50s catalogs and magazines.

Duty Now for the Future
DEVO
Cover art: Janet Perr
Warner Bros., 1979

Oh, No! It's Devo
DEVO
Cover art: Devo/Rick Seireeni
Photography: Erik Arnesen
Warner Bros., 1982

THE PSYCHEDELIC FURS

TALK • TALK • TALK

26

Talk Talk Talk
THE PSYCHEDELIC FURS
Cover art: Unknown
Photography: Andrew Douglas
Columbia/CBS, 1981

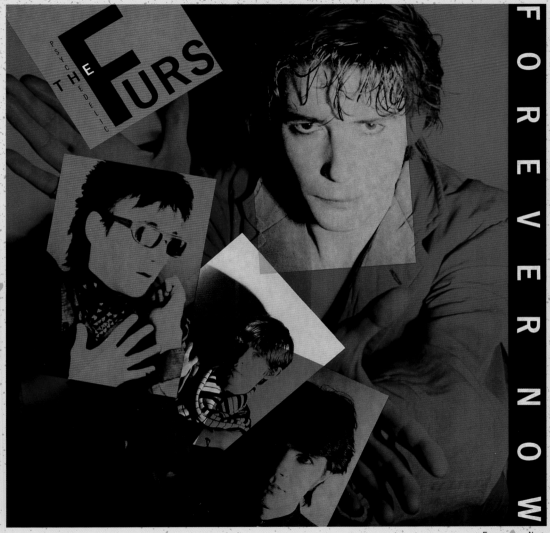

PSYCHEDELIC THE FURS

FOREVER NOW

27

Forever Now
THE PSYCHEDELIC FURS
Cover art: Chris Austopchuck
Photography: Marcia Resnick/Antoine Giacomoni
Columbia/CBS, 1982

HIGH FIDELITY

the B-52's

THE B-52'S
Cover Art: Sue Ab Surd
Photography: George DuBose
Warner Bros., 1979

The B-52's retro style is the "cover art" on this, their first album and Wild Planet, their second.

29

Wild Planet
THE B-52'S
Cover art: Robert Waldrop
Photography: Lynn Goldsmith
Warner Bros., 1980

Peter Gabriel (II)
PETER GABRIEL
Cover art: Hipgnosis
Atlantic, 1978

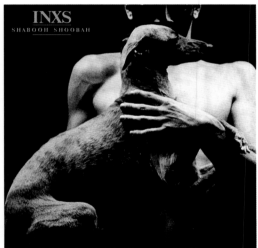

Shabooh Shoobah
INXS
Cover art: Grant Mathews/Michael Hutchence
Photography: Grant Mathews
Atco, 1982

JOE JACKSON

I'M THE MAN

31

I'm the Man
JOE JACKSON
Cover art: Joe Jackson/Michael Ross
Photography: Bruce Rae
A&M, 1979

OINGO BOINGO
Cover art: Carl Grasso/Louis Wain
I.R.S., 1980

Only A Lad
OINGO BOINGO
Cover art: Chuck Beeson/Paul Mussa/Chris Hopkins
I.R.S./A&M, 1981

PRETENDERS

34

PRETENDERS
Cover art: Kevin Hughes
Photography: Chalkie Davies
Sire, 1980

Pretenders II
PRETENDERS
Cover art: Gavin Cochrane
Real/Sire, 1981

Sundown
RANK AND FILE
Cover art: Sam Yeates/Jeff Price
Slash, 1982

A FLOCK OF SEAGULLS
Cover art: Pete Watson
Jive/Arista, 1981

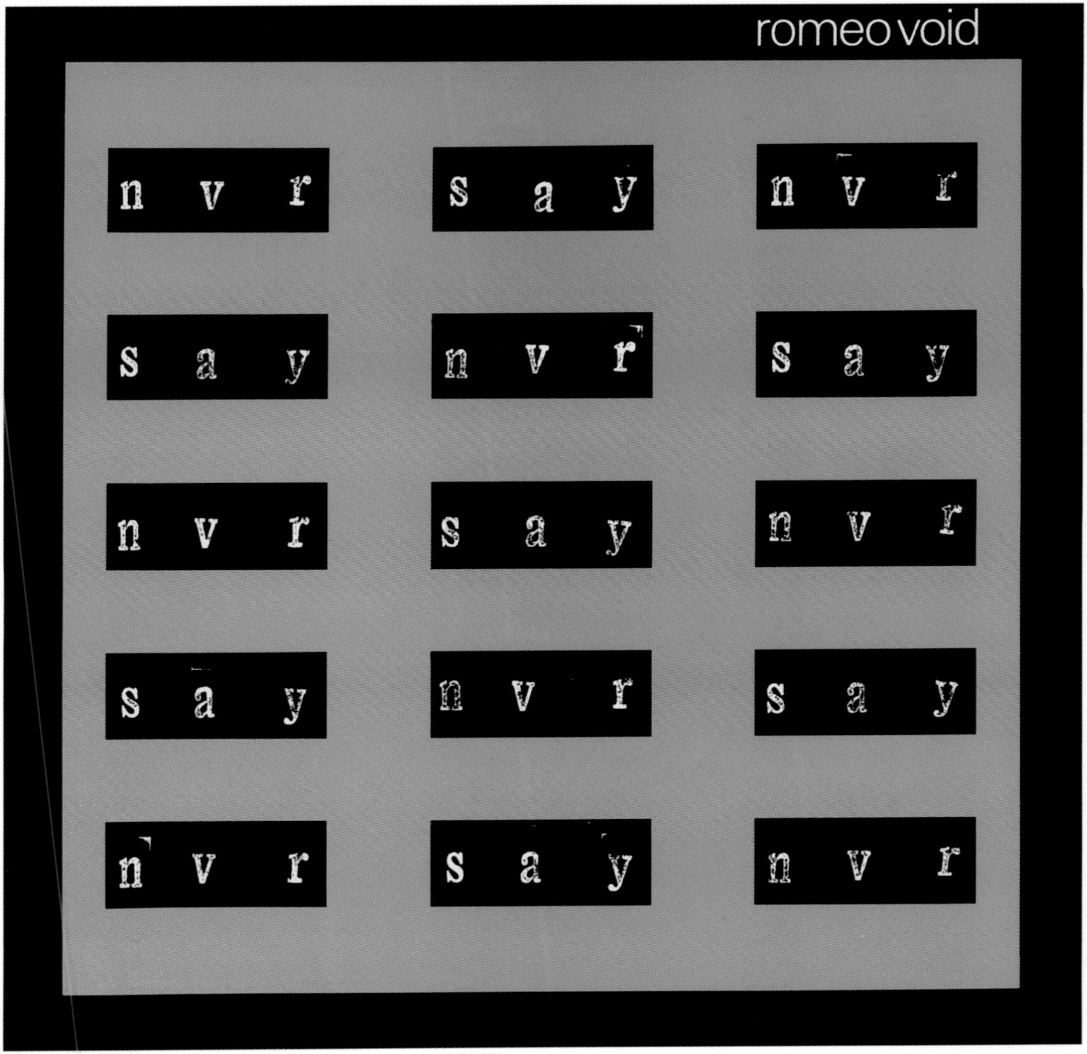

Never Say Never
ROMEO VOID
Cover art: Frank Zincavage/Peter Soe, Jr.
415/CBS, 1981

37

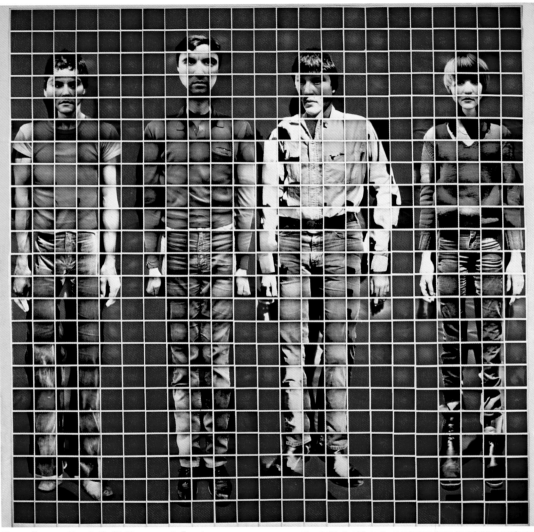

38

More Songs About Buildings and Food
TALKING HEADS
Cover art: David Byrne/Jimmy de Sana
Sire, 1978

Conceived by David Byrne, the cover for More Songs About Buildings and Food *is a photomosaic made up of 529 Polaroids.*

URBAN VERBS

URBAN VERBS
Cover art: Urban Verbs
Photography: Christopher West/Freddie Leiberman
Warner Bros., 1980

Power Corruption and Lies
NEW ORDER
Cover art: Peter Saville/Fantin La Tour
Rough Trade, 1981

Wilder
THE TEARDROP EXPLODES
Cover Art: Martyn Atkins
Mercury/Phonogram, 1981

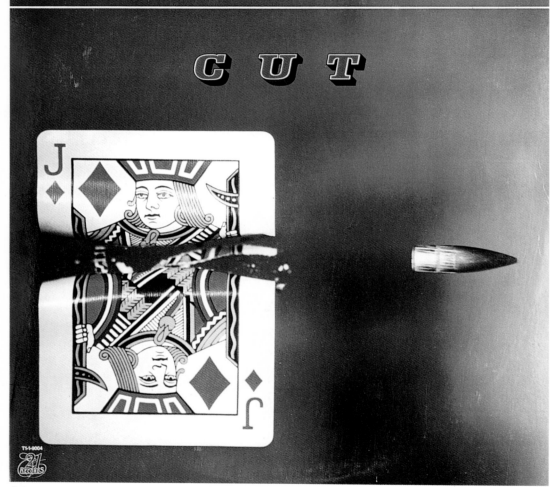

42

Cut
GOLDEN EARRING
Cover art: Unknown
21/PolyGram, 1982

ORCHESTRAL MANŒUVRES IN THE DARK

CRUSH

43

Crush
ORCHESTRAL MANOEUVRES IN THE DARK
Cover art: Paul Slater/XL Design
Virgin, 1985

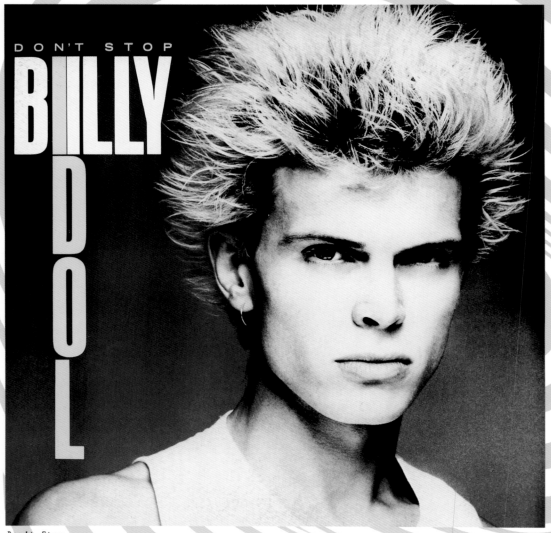

44

DON'T STOP
**BILLY
IDOL**

Don't Stop
BILLY IDOL
Cover art: Janet Levinson
Photography: Brian Aris
Chrysalis, 1981

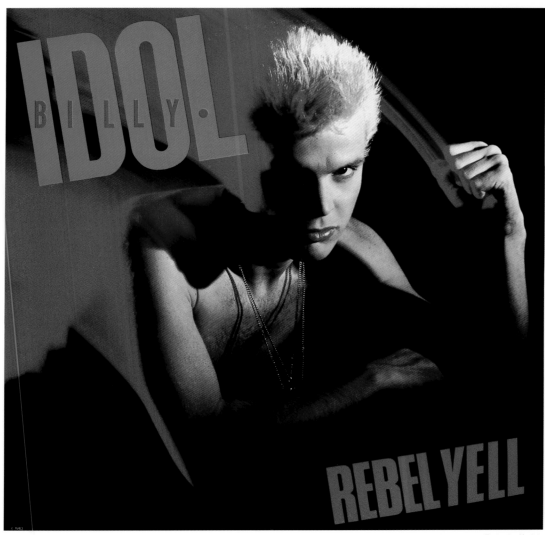

45

Rebel Yell
BILLY IDOL
Cover art: Michael McNeil
Photography: Brian Griffin
Chrysalis, 1983

LIVING IN THE PLASTIC AGE ═══ **VIDEO KILLED THE RADIO-STAR** ═══ **KID DYNAMO** ═══ **I LOVE YOU (MISS ROBOT)**

BUGGLES
THE AGE OF   PLASTIC

The Age of Plastic
THE BUGGLES
Cover art: Unknown
Island, 1980

The Buggles' only hit was the MTV anthem "Video Killed the Radio Star."

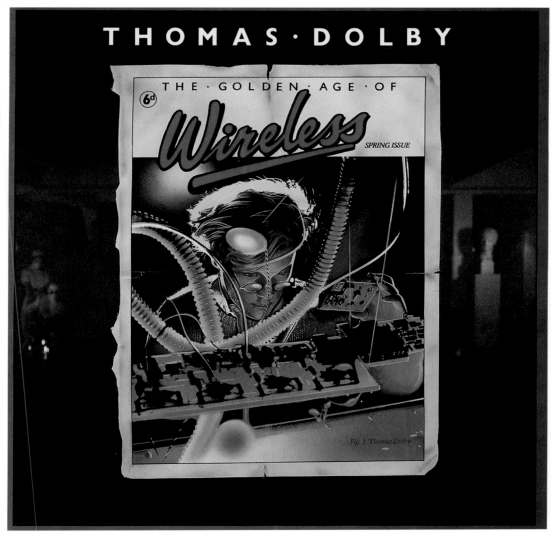

The Golden Age of Wireless
THOMAS DOLBY
Cover art: Thomas Dolby/Andrew Douglas/Bill Smith
Venice in Peril/Capitol, 1983

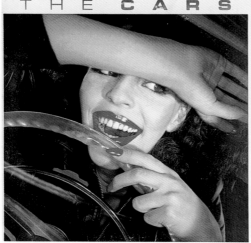

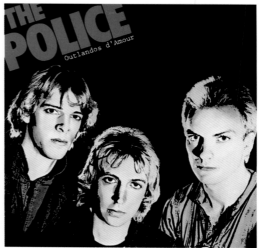

THE CARS
Cover Art: Ron Coro/Johnny Lee
Photography: Elliot Gilbert
Elektra/Asylum, 1978

Outlandos d'Amour
THE POLICE
Cover art: Michael Ross
Photography: Janette Beckman
A&M, 1979

*While most New Wave albums can still be found for $20 or less, due to '80s
release gimmickry many fetch much larger amounts. In 1983 the Police released a
limited pressing picture-disc of Ghost in the Machine that lights up when played.
This record is now worth around $1000.*

APPROVED BY

THE MOTORS

INCLUDES THE HITS
"AIRPORT"
"FORGET ABOUT YOU"
"TODAY"

49

Approved by the Motors
THE MOTORS
Cover art: Hipgnosis/Hardie
Virgin, 1978

50

SYLVAIN SYLVAIN
Cover art: Katsuji Asada
Photography: Toshi
RCA, 1979

Syl Sylvain was a member of the revolutionary New York Dolls.

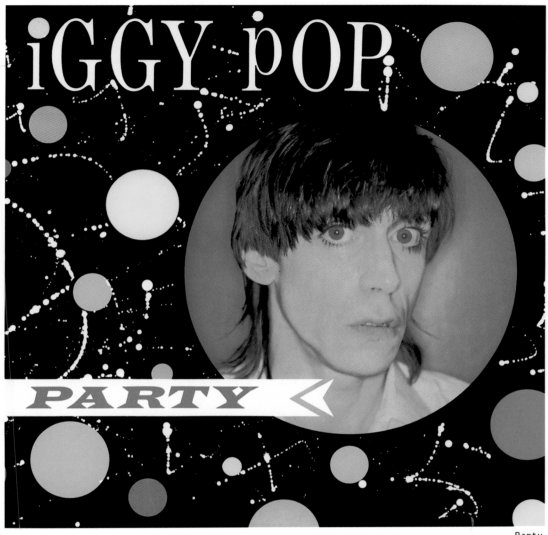

51

Party
IGGY POP
Cover art: Unknown
Arista, 1981

TELEVISION

MARQUEE MOON

Marquee Moon
TELEVISION
Cover art: Tony Lane
Photography: Robert Mapplethorpe
Elektra/Asylum, 1977

This is a RECORD COVER. This writing is the DESIGN upon the record cover. The DESIGN is to help SELL the record. We hope to draw your attention to it and encourage you to pick it up. When you have done that maybe you'll be persuaded to listen to the music - in this case XTC's Go 2 album. Then we want you to BUY it. The idea being that the more of you that buy this record the more money Virgin Records, the manager Ian Reid and XTC themselves will make. To the aforementioned this is known as PLEASURE. A good cover DESIGN is one that attracts more buyers and gives more pleasure. This writing is trying to pull you in much like an eye-catching picture. It is designed to get you to READ IT. This is called luring the VICTIM, and you are the VICTIM. But if you have a free mind you should STOP READING NOW! because all we are attempting to do is to get you to read on. Yet this is a DOUBLE BIND because if you indeed stop you'll be doing what we tell you, and if you read on you'll be doing what we've wanted all along. And the more you read on the more you're falling for this simple device of telling you exactly how a good commercial design works. They're TRICKS and this is the worst TRICK of all since it's describing the TRICK whilst trying to TRICK you, and if you've read this far then you're TRICKED but you wouldn't have known this unless you'd read this far. At least we're telling you directly instead of seducing you with a beautiful or haunting visual that may never tell you. We're letting you know that you ought to buy this record because in essence it's a PRODUCT and PRODUCTS are to be consumed and you are a consumer and this is a good PRODUCT. We could have written the band's name in special lettering so that it stood out and you'd see it before you'd read any of this writing and possibly have bought it anyway. What we are really suggesting is that you are FOOLISH to buy or not buy an album merely as a consequence of the design on its cover. This is a con because if you agree then you'll probably like this writing - which is the cover design - and hence the album inside. But we've just warned you against that. The con is a con. A good cover design could be considered as one that gets you to buy the record, but that never actually happens to YOU because YOU know it's just a design for the cover. And this is the RECORD COVER.

53

Influenced by punk's questioning of the status quo, design firm Hipgnosis, challenged the very idea and purpose of album cover art on Go 2's cover: "The DESIGN is to help SELL the record . . . But if you have a free mind, you should STOP READING NOW!"

Go 2
XTC
Cover art: Hipgnosis
Virgin, 1978

54

ROXY MUSIC
Cover art: Bryan Ferry/Nicholas de Ville
Photography: Karl Stoecker
Reprise/Island, 1972
Atco/Polydor, 1976

Roxy Music's campy first cover features the idealized fan, a personification of femi-
nine desirability. According to Nicholas de Ville, who collaborated on the cover, the
woman represents a Roxy Music fan, who by symbiotic magic, gives status to the
band. The greater the fan's status—the more glamourous her persona—the more
exalted is the band of which she is the fan.

Country Life
ROXY MUSIC
Cover art: Nicholas de Ville/Bryan Ferry/Bob Bowkett
Photography: Eric Boman
Atco/Island, 1974

Country Life
ROXY MUSIC
Cover art: Nicholas de Ville/Bryan Ferry/Bob Bowkett
Photography: Eric Boman
Atco/Island, 1974

Because of the risqué cover, many retailers in America refused to stock Country Life. Atlantic Records disguised some of the LPs with green shrink-wrap and pressed an alternative cover that removed the women altogether.

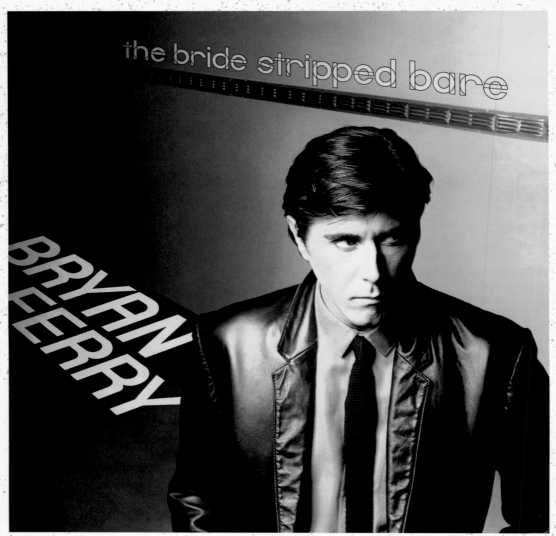

the bride stripped bare

BRYAN FERRY

56

The Bride Stripped Bare
BRYAN FERRY
Cover art: Antony Price/Cream/Brian Harris
Photography: John Swannell
Atlantic/Polydor, 1978

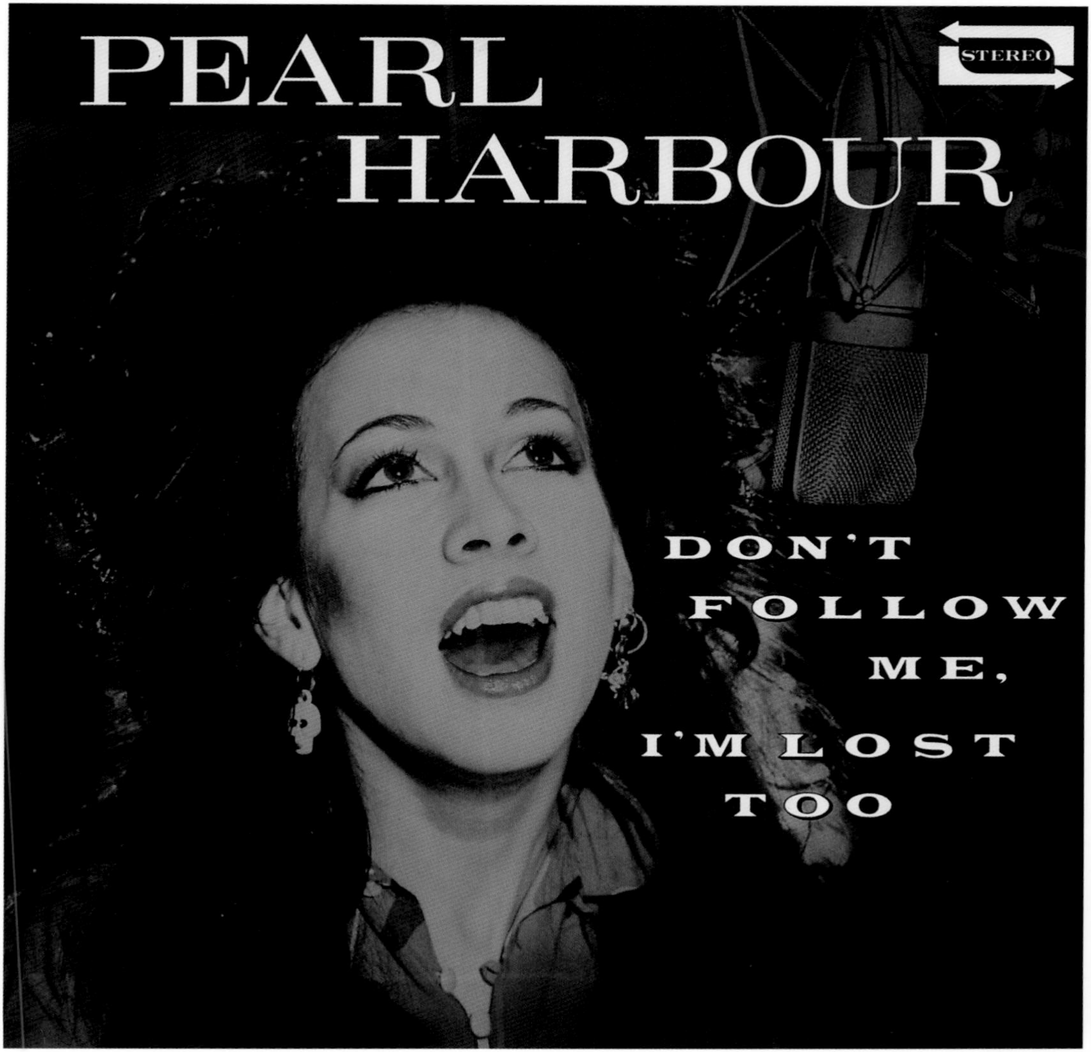

PEARL HARBOUR

STEREO

DON'T
FOLLOW
ME,
I'M LOST
TOO

57

Don't Follow Me, I'm Lost Too
PEARL HARBOUR
Cover art: Unknown
Warner Bros., 1980

DO IT YOURSELF

IAN DURY
& the
BLOCKHEADS

SIDE ONE	SIDE TWO
INBETWEENIES	THIS IS WHAT WE FIND
QUIET ➡	UNEASY SUNNY DAY HOTSY TOTSY
DON'T ASK ME	MISCHIEF
SINK MY BOATS	⬅ DANCE OF THE SCREAMERS
WAITING FOR YOUR TAXI	LULLABY FOR FRANCES

Do It Yourself
IAN DURY & THE BLOCKHEADS
Cover art: Barney Bubbles
Photography: Chris Gabrin
Stiff-Epic, 1979

Do It Yourself was printed with 28 different wallpaper backgrounds.

Lord Upminster
IAN DURY
Cover art: Unknown
Photography: Paul Kaye
Polydor, 1981

Labour of Lust
NICK LOWE
Cover art: Unknown
Columbia, 1979

Many English New Wavers, such as Nick Lowe, played in the early '70s pub-rock bands.

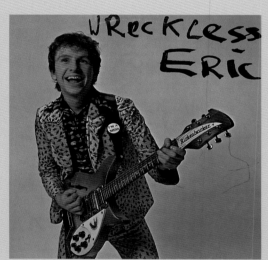

Subtle as A Flying Mallet
DAVE EDMUNDS
Cover art: Hipgnosis
RCA, 1975

WRECKLESS ERIC
Cover art: Unknown
Stiff, 1978

JONATHAN RICHMAN & THE MODERN LOVERS
Photography: Fabian Bachrach
Beserkley, 1976

62

Robert Fripp Exposure

Exposure
ROBERT FRIPP
Cover art: Chris Stein
E.G./Polydor, 1979

Robert Fripp produced such New Wave artists as Blondie, Peter Gabriel, and Talking Heads.

New Clear Days
THE VAPORS
Cover art: Paul Briginshaw/John Pasche
Photography: Phil Jude
Liberty/United, 1980

GANG OF FOUR
entertainment!

'The Indian smiles, he thinks that the cowboy is his friend.

The cowboy smiles, he is glad the Indian is fooled.

Now he can exploit him.

Entertainment!
GANG OF FOUR
Cover art: Jon King/Andy Gill/Cream
Warner Bros., 1979

Songs of the Free
GANG OF FOUR
Cover art: Shoot That Tiger!
Photography: Colin Barker
Warner Bros., 1982

the telefones

vibration change

Vibration Change
THE TELEFONES
Cover art: Daisy Dillon/Hector Acevedo/Cliff Bott
VVV, 1980

TALKING HEADS
FEAR OF MUSIC

67

Fear of Music
TALKING HEADS
Cover art: Jerry Harrison
Sire, 1979

No Wave
COMPILATION
Cover art: Chuck Beeson/Lou Beach/Katherine Walter
A&M, 1978

Thru the Back Door
COMPILATION
Cover art: Joe Kotleba
Photography: Jim Matusik
Mercury/Phonogram, 1980

Wanna Buy a Bridge?
COMPILATION
Cover art: Unknown
Rough Trade, 1980

NICK LOWE

PURE POP FOR NOW PEOPLE

Pure Pop For Now People
NICK LOWE
Cover art: Barney Bubbles
Columbia, 1978

Pure Pop for Now People *was titled* Jesus of Cool *in the U.K. and featured variations in photographs. The British version did not include Lowe sporting an American flag tie.*

YIPES!
Cover art: Unknown
Millennium, 1979

Too-Rye-Ay
KEVIN ROWLAND &
DEXYS MIDNIGHT RUNNERS
Cover art: Peter Barrett/Kim Knott/Andrew Ratcliffe
Phonogram, 1982

FINGERPRINTZ

"DISTINGUISHING MARKS"

Distinguishing Marks
FINGERPRINTZ
Cover art: Peter Saville/John Stalin
Virgin, 1980

Designed by Peter Saville, the cover for Distinguishing Marks features perforated cards with illustrations reminiscent of pulp fiction covers.

BA-253 200180

73

COMATEENS

COMATEENS
Cover art: Claude Paparella
Photography: Joe Stevens
Call Me, 1981

74

Pressure
BRAM TCHAIKOVSKY
Cover art: Rockin' Russian
Radarscope, 1980

Released in the UK under the title The Russians are Coming, Rockin' Russian's
cover borrows from the graphics of Russian Revolutionary art.

YACHTS
Cover art: Able Images
Photography: Tom Sheehan
Radarscope, 1979

Without Radar
YACHTS
Cover art: Malcom Garrett
Photography: Chris Gabrin
Radarscope, 1980

In a Place Like This
PAYOLA$
Cover art: James O'Mara
I.R.S./A&M, 1981

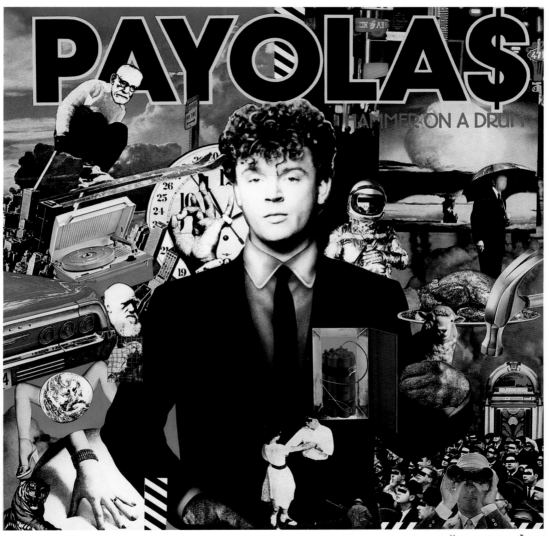

Hammer on a Drum
PAYOLA$
Cover art: David Andoff/Matthew Wiley
I.R.S./A&M, 1983

The Swimming Pool Q's

The deep end.

The Deep End
THE SWIMMING POOL Q'S
Cover art: Anne Richmond Boston
DB, 1981

78

ANIMOTION
Cover art: Bill Levy/SteeleWorks
Mercury, 1984

80

Teenage Depression
EDDIE AND THE HOT RODS
Cover art: Michael Beal
Island, 1976

Music for Pleasure
THE DAMNED
Cover art: Barney Bubbles/Phil Smee
Stiff, 1977

82

Thin Red Line
THE CRETONES
Cover art: Kosh
Photography: Aaron Rapoport
Planet, 1980

"Kosh" was John Kosh, who also designed covers for the Motels and The Eagles' Hotel California.

Snap! Snap!
THE CRETONES
Cover art: Neon Park/Ron Coro/Floyd Uyehara
Planet, 1981

the iNMaTES

FiRST OFFENCE

84

First Offence
THE INMATES
Cover art: Malcom Garrett/Tim Read
Photography: Sheila Rock
Radarscope, 1979

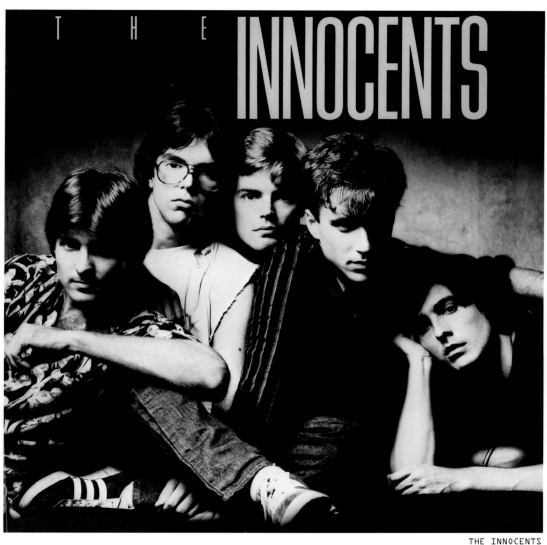

THE INNOCENTS

85

THE INNOCENTS
Cover art: Jeff Lancaster/Art Hotel
Photography: Norman Seeff
Boardwalk, 1982

86

THE ROMANTICS
Cover art: Unknown
Nemperor, 1979

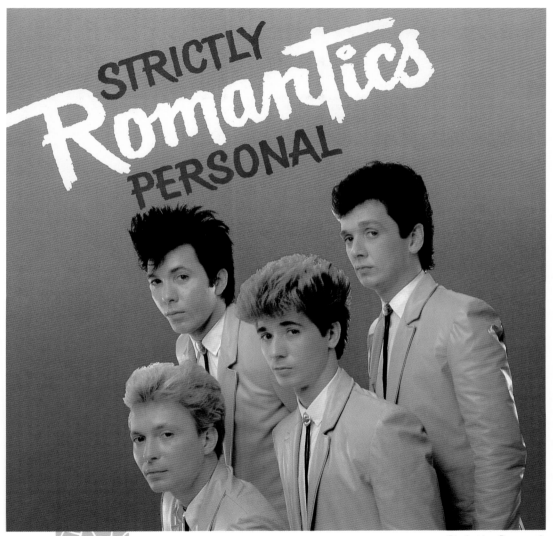

Strictly Personal
THE ROMANTICS
Cover art: Alex Marinos
Photography: Michael Halsband
Nemperor/Epic, 1981

88

NERVUS REX
Cover art: Glenn Ross/Tim Owens/Dianne Athey
Photography: Moshe Brakha
Dreamland, 1980

THE MEMBERS

U P R H Y T H M, D O W N B E A T

89

Uprhythm, Downbeat
THE MEMBERS
Cover art: Howard Fritzson
Photography: David Stetson
Arista, 1982

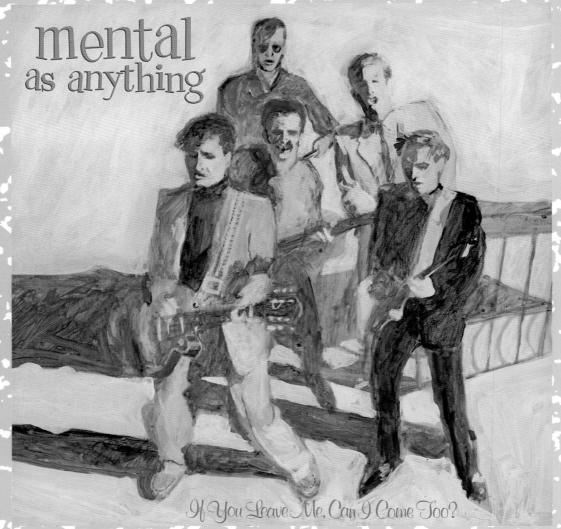

mental
as anything

90

If You Leave Me, Can I Come Too?

If You Leave Me, Can I Come Too?
MENTAL AS ANYTHING
Cover art: Unknown
A&M, 1982

NAKED EYES
Cover art: Henry E. Marquez/Patty Dryden
EMI America, 1983

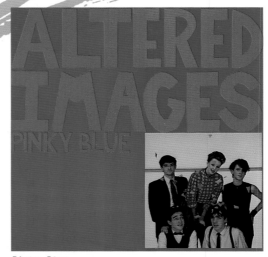

The Sound of the Suburbs (Single)
THE MEMBERS
Cover art: Unknown
Virgin, 1979

Pinky Blue
ALTERED IMAGES
Cover art: Unknown
Portrait/CBS, 1982

BITE
ALTERED IMAGES

Cover designer Martyn Atkins worked with Peter Saville at Manchester's Factory Records. He would later form his own firm, Town and Country Planning.

Bite
ALTERED IMAGES
Cover art: Altered Images/Martyn Atkins
Photography: Neil Kirk
Portrait/CBS, 1983

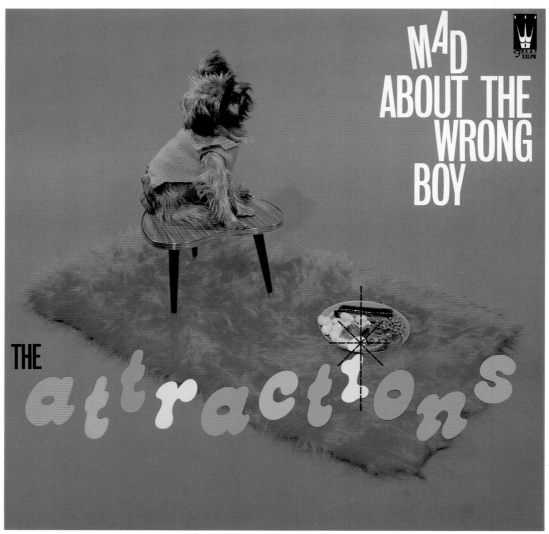

MAD
ABOUT THE
WRONG
BOY

THE *attractions*

94

Mad About the Wrong Boy
THE ATTRACTIONS
Cover art: Barney Bubbles
Photography: Brian Griffin
F-Beat, 1980

The Attractions were Elvis Costello's back-up band.

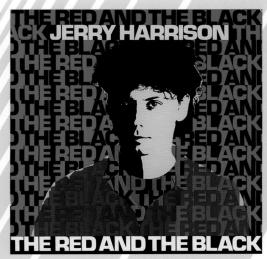

Remain in Light
TALKING HEADS
Cover art: M & Co.
Sire, 1980

The Red and the Black
JERRY HARRISON
Cover art: Chris Callis/Jerry Harrison
Sire, 1981

Mirror Stars
FABULOUS POODLES
Cover art: Hipgnosis
Park Lane/Epic, 1978

*The trend-setting design firm Hipgnosis is best known for its Pink Floyd covers,
including Dark Side of the Moon. Members of the firm, Storm Thorgerson and
Aubrey Powell, were once roommates of Pink Floyd's Syd Barrett.*

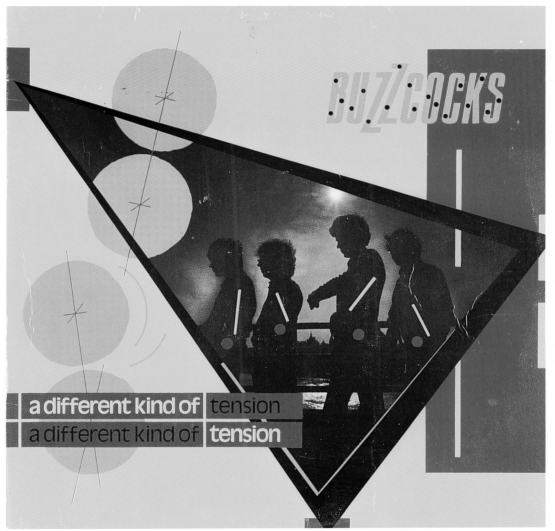

Malcom Garrett designed many covers for the Buzzcocks. The relationship began while he was still in design school at Manchester Polytechnic where he met the band's manager, Richard Boon.

A Different Kind of Tension
BUZZCOCKS
Cover art: Malcom Garrett
Photography: Jill Furmanovsky
I.R.S./Liberty-United, 1980

Pelican West
HAIRCUT ONE HUNDRED
Cover art: Nick Heyward/David Shortt/Peter Hill
Photography: Gered Mankowitz
Arista, 1982

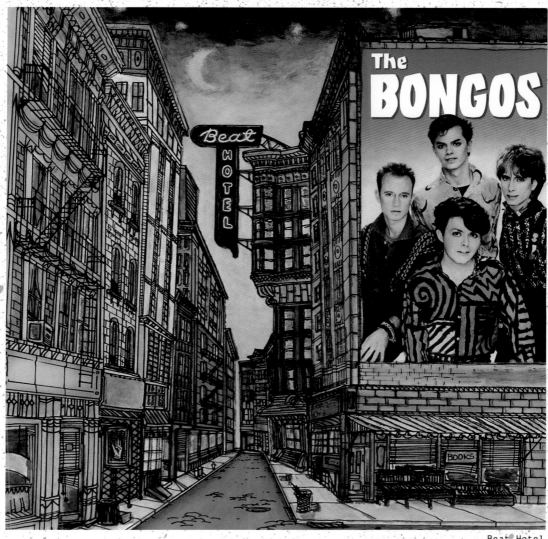

99

Beat Hotel
THE BONGOS
Cover art: Unknown
RCA, 1985

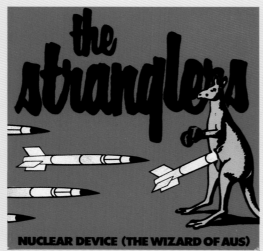

Nuclear Device (Single)
THE STRANGLERS
Cover art: Unknown
Liberty/United, 1979

My Perfect Cousin (Single)
THE UNDERTONES
Cover art: Unknown
Sire, 1980

THE **UNDERTONES**
THE **SIN OF PRIDE**

The Sin of Pride
THE UNDERTONES
Cover art: Willie Doherty
Photography: Rob Brimson/Willie Doherty
Ardeck, 1983

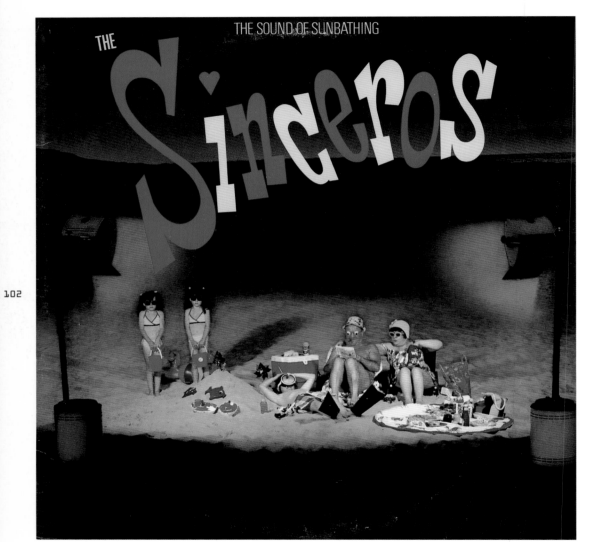

The Sound of Sunbathing
THE SINCEROS
Cover art: Andrea Klein
Photography: Benno Friedman
Columbia, 1970

HUMAN SEXUAL RESPONSE

Fig. 14

Hipgnosis covers often featured surreal scenes, borrowing from artists such as Dali and Magritte.

Fig. 14
HUMAN SEXUAL RESPONSE
Cover art: Hipgnosis/Paul Maxon
Eat-Passport, 1980

104

THE HEATERS
Cover art: William Wray
Ariola, 1978

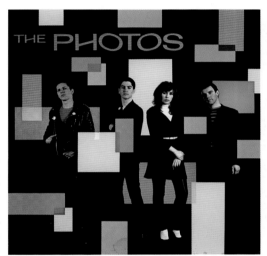

THE PHOTOS
Cover art: Keith Breeden
Photography: Chris Gabrin
Epic, 1980

Coup de Grace
MINK DE VILLE
Cover art: Bob Defrin/Sandi Young
Photography: John Pilgreen
Atlantic, 1981

The Photos' cover designer Keith Breeden worked for Malcom Garrett in his firm Assorted Images.

ELVIS COSTELLO

MY AIM IS TRUE

My Aim Is True
ELVIS COSTELLO
Cover art: Barney Bubbles
Photography: Keith Morris
Stiff, 1977

The Stiff release of My Aim Is True featured a black-and white photograph. In later versions, the background is yellow. The cover was designed by Barney Bubbles, who also created several Stiff logos.

Trust
ELVIS COSTELLO AND THE ATTRACTIONS
Cover art: Unknown
F-Beat/Columbia Records, 1981

Imperial Bedroom
ELVIS COSTELLO AND THE ATTRACTIONS
Cover art: Barney Bubbles/Sal Forlenza
Columbia/F-Beat, 1982

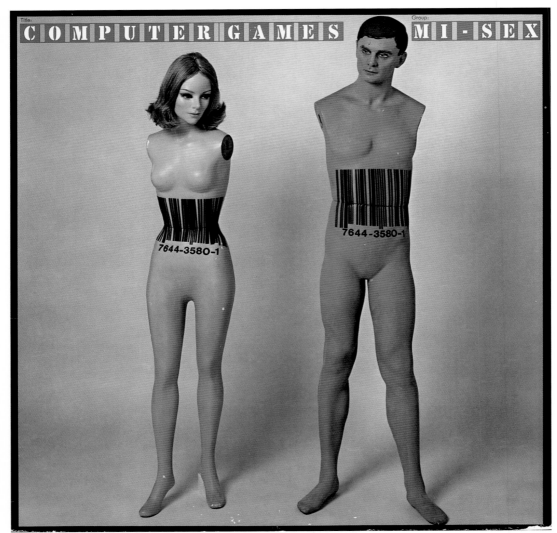

Computer Games
MI-SEX
Cover art: Janet Perr/Paula Scher
Photography: Arnold Rosenberg
Epic, 1979

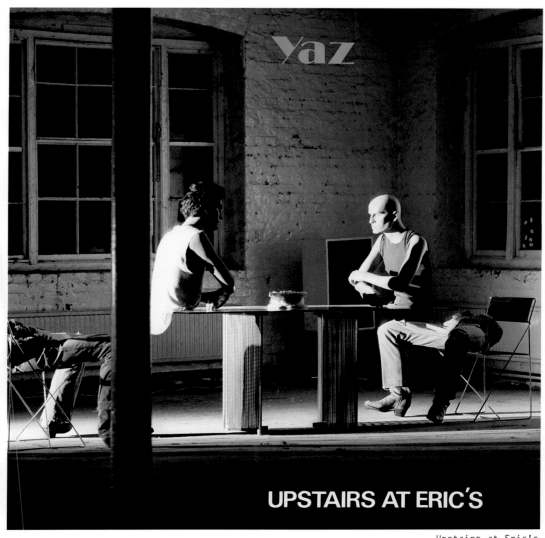

yaz

UPSTAIRS AT ERIC'S

109

Upstairs at Eric's
YAZ
Cover art: Joe Lyons
Sire/Mute, 1982

A Tonic for the Troops
THE BOOMTOWN RATS
Cover art: Hothouse/Chuck Loyola
Photography: Fin Costello
Columbia, 1978

Music for Parties
SILICON TEENS
Cover art: Simone Grant
Mute/Sire, 1980

111

Happy Families
BLANCMANGE
Cover art: Michael Brownlow
London, 1982

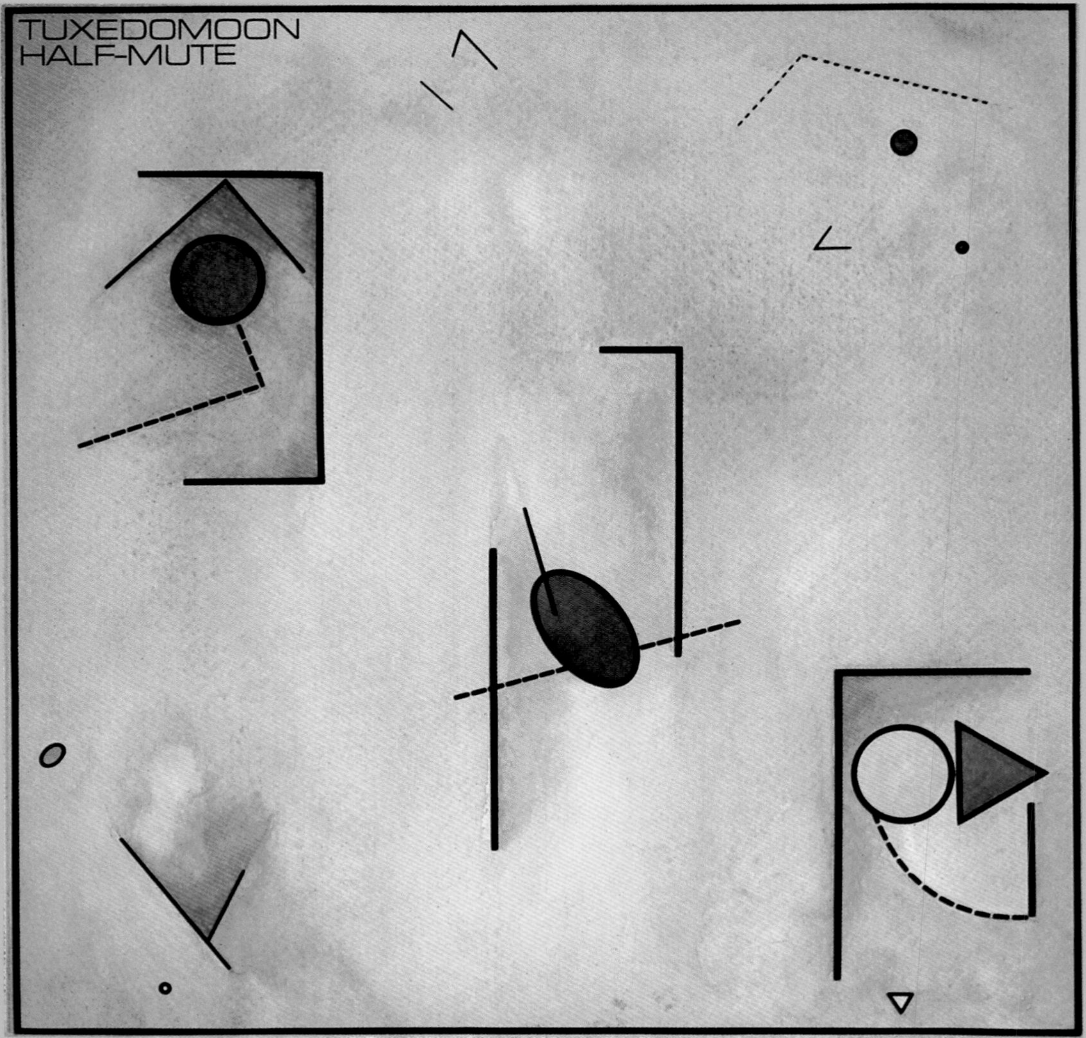

TUXEDOMOON
HALF-MUTE

112

Half-Mute
TUXEDOMOON
Cover Art: Patrick Roques
Crammed Discs, 1979

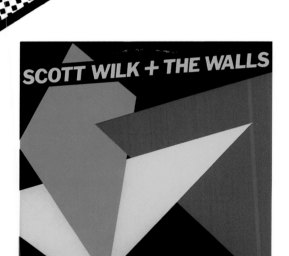

SCOTT WILK + THE WALLS
Cover art: Unknown
Warner Bros., 1980

Digital Stimulation
UNITS
Cover art: Rachel Webber
415, 1980

Vibing Up the Senile Man
ALTERNATIVE TV
Cover art: Jill Furmanovsky
Deptford Fun City, 1979

Sector 27
TOM ROBINSON
Cover art: Unknown
I.R.S., 1980

YELLOW MAGIC ORCHESTRA
Cover art: Lou Beach/Roland Young/Amy Nagasawa/Chuck Beeson
Horizon/A&M, 1979

Pop Art
ELTON MOTELLO
Cover art: Elton Motello/Mark Sevrin/Michael Sprimont
Passport, 1980

Playing with a Different Sex
AU PAIRS
Cover art: Martin/Rockin' Russian
Photography: Eve Arnold
Human, 1981

THE DEL-BYZANTEENS

LIES TO LIVE BY

The title track on The Del-Byzanteens' Lies to Live By was featured in Wim Wenders' film The State of Things. The band included future film director Jim Jarmusch on keyboards.

Lies to Live By
THE DEL-BYZANTEENS
Cover art: Philippe Hagen
Don't Fall Off the Mountain, 1982

KILLING JOKE

what's THIS for...!

What's This For...!
KILLING JOKE
Cover art: Unknown
Editions EG/Malicious Damage, 1981

Born to Laugh at Tornadoes
WAS (NOT WAS)
Cover art: Jeri McManus/Dan Chapman
ZE/Geffen, 1983

WAS (NOT WAS)

BORN TO LAUGH AT TORNADOES

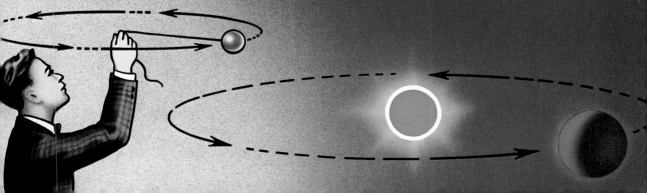

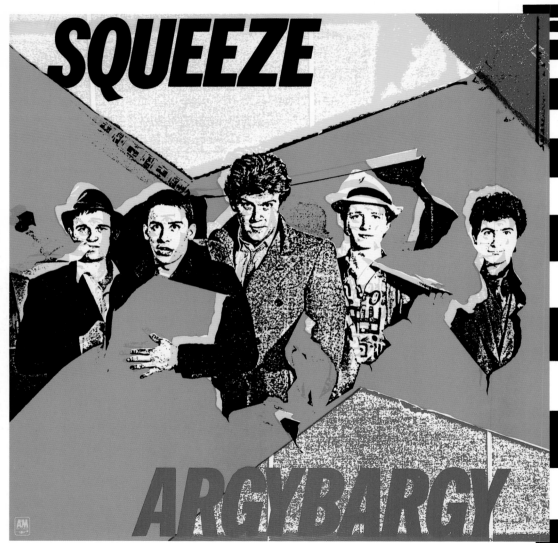

120

Argybargy
SQUEEZE
Cover art: Michael Ross
Photography: Mike Laye
A&M, 1980

Take Me, I'm Yours (Single)
SQUEEZE
Cover art: Nick Marshall/Michael Ross
Photography: George Greenwood
Rondor/A&M, 1978

Cosi Fan Tutti Frutti
SQUEEZE
Cover art: Michael Ross/Rob O'Connor/Simon Fell
A&M, 1985

122

Ha!Ha!Ha!
ULTRAVOX
Cover art: Dennis Leigh/Bloomfield and Travis
Island, 1977

The cover for Ha! Ha! Ha! explores creative manipulations in the printing process,
purposefully misregistering color plates. A similar effect can be seen on Squeeze's
cover for Argybargy.

ULTRAVOX

123

QUARTET

Quartet
ULTRAVOX
Cover art: Peter Saville Associates/Ken Kennedy
Chrysalis, 1983

124

Sound-On-Sound
BILL NELSON'S RED NOISE
Cover art: Cream
Photography: Bishin Jumonji
EMI, 1979

The Modern Dance
PERE UBU
Cover art: S. W. Taylor
Rough Trade, 1981

ABC ★★★

SRM-1-4059 ℗ mercury

OAD N.W.3

126

the
Lexicon
of Love

a-z affectionately, 1 to 10 alphabetically, from here to eternity without
in betweens. still looking for a custom fit in an off the rack world?
sales talk from sales assistants when all i want to do is lower your
resistance. no rhythm in cymbals no tempo in drums. love's on
arrival, she comes when she comes. right on the target but wide of the…

The Lexicon of Love
ABC
Cover art: ABC/Visible Ink
Photography: Gered Mankowitz
Mercury/Neutron, 1982

ABC's lead, Martin Fry, contributed to the look of many of the band's covers,
including The Lexicon of Love, which is an ode to old-fashioned over-the-top
romanticism.

For Beauty Stab, designer Keith Breeden re-created a low-brow bull/matador painting.

Beauty Stab
ABC
Cover art: ABC/Keith Breeden
Mercury/Phonogram, 1983

THE WAITRESSES

Wasn't Tomorrow Wonderful?

Wasn't Tomorrow Wonderful?
THE WAITRESSES
Cover art: Andrew Fuhrmann/Chris Butler
Photography: George DuBose
ZE/PolyGram, 1982

The Waitresses were part of the Akron, Ohio, music scene, home to many New Wave bands, including Jane Aire and the Belvederes, Devo, and Rachel Sweet.

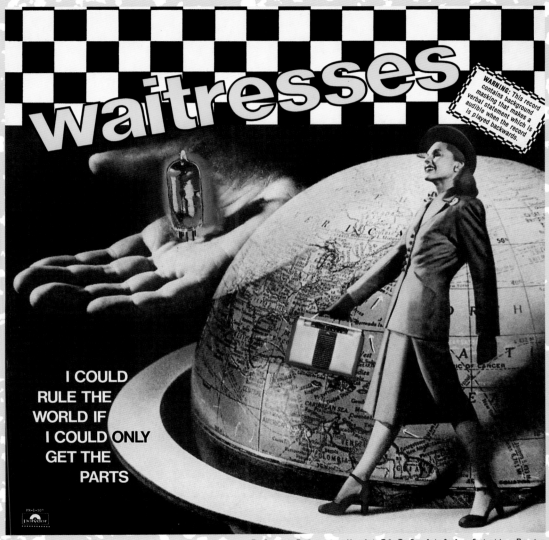

WARNING: This record contains background masking that makes a verbal statement which is audible when the record is played backwards.

waitresses

I COULD
RULE THE
WORLD IF
I COULD ONLY
GET THE
PARTS

129

I Could Rule the World If I Could Only Get the Parts
WAITRESSES
Cover art: Ed Caraeff/Zox
Polydor, 1982

New Love
METRO
Cover art: Cream
EMI, 1979

Space Race
MI-SEX
Cover art: Mi-Sex/Ian McCausland
Epic, 1980

New York*London*Paris*Munich
M
Cover art: Stan Kerr
Sire, 1979

132

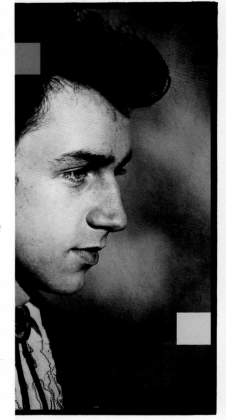

Who? What? When? Where? Why?
WEIRDOS
Cover art: Unknown
Bomp, 1979

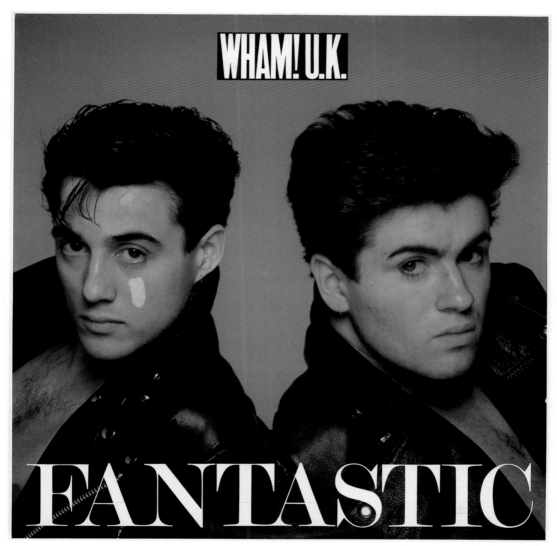

WHAM! U.K.

FANTASTIC

Fantastic
WHAM! U.K.
Cover art: Unknown
Innervision/Columbia, 1982

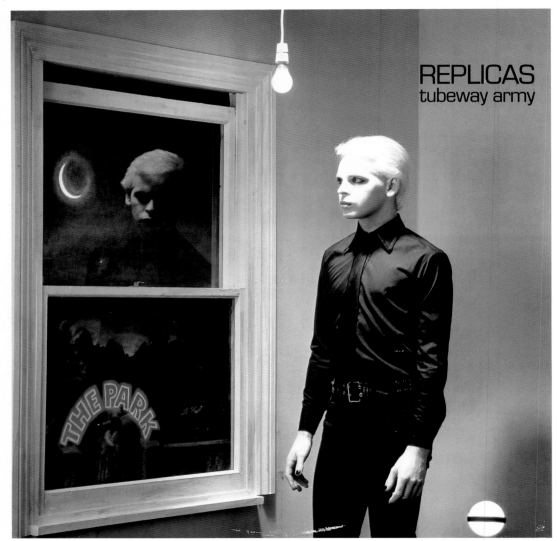

REPLICAS
tubeway army

134

Replicas' synthesizer dance hit "Are Friends Electric?" reached No. 1 in the U.K.

Replicas
TUBEWAY ARMY
Cover art: Malti Kidia/Tony Escott
Photography: Geoff Howes
Beggars Banquet, 1979

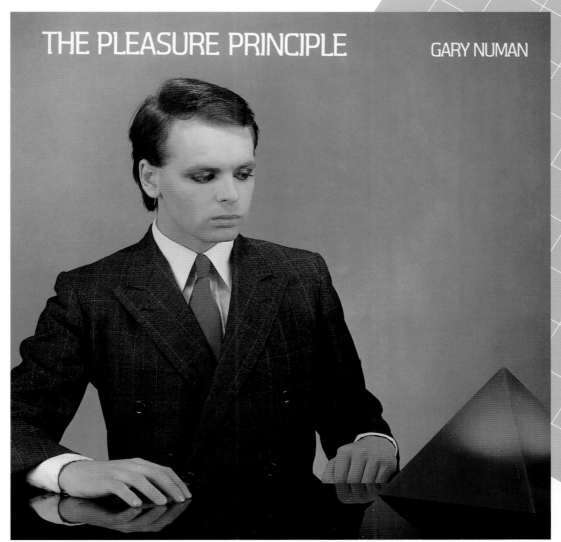

THE PLEASURE PRINCIPLE

GARY NUMAN

135

The Pleasure Principle
GARY NUMAN
Cover art: Malti Kidia
Photography: Geoff Howes
Beggars Banquet/Atco, 1979

THE TOURISTS

LUMINOUS BASEMENT

136

Luminous Basement
THE TOURISTS
Cover art: Willy Smax
RCA, 1980

Members of the Tourists, Annie Lennox and Dave Stewart, formed Eurythmics.

RCA

EURYTHMICS
in the Garden

Al McDowell formed the British design firm Rockin' Russian. In 1980, McDowell,
along with ex-art director of Vogue, Terry Jones, started i-D magazine.

In the Garden
EURYTHMICS
Cover art: Rockin' Russian
Photography: Peter Ashworth
RCA, 1981

Black Snake Diamond Role
ROBYN HITCHCOCK
Cover art: Unknown
Go International, 1981

Big Science
LAURIE ANDERSON
Cover art: Perry Hoberman/Cindy Brown
Photography: Greg Shifrin
Warner Bros., 1982

Tin Drum
JAPAN
Cover art: D. Sylvian/Steve Joule
Photography: Fin Costello
Virgin, 1981

THE CHURCH
Cover art: Roy Kohara/Peter Shea/Paul Patte
Capitol, 1982

Malcom Garrett designed several Simple Minds covers, including New Gold Dream and Sparkle in the Rain. The typography and design of both evoke the Saxon and Celtic culture and sounds the band was exploring at the time.

New Gold Dream
SIMPLE MINDS
Cover art: Malcom Garrett/Assorted Images
Virgin, 1982

The Bible of Bop
KIMBERLEY REW
Cover art: Unknown
Compendium Incorporated, 1982

KATRINA AND THE WAVES
Cover art: Manhattan Design/Pat Gorman
Photography: Caroline Greyshock
Capitol, 1985

KATRINA AND THE WAVES

143

Waves
KATRINA AND THE WAVES
Cover art: Stylo Rouge
Photography: Simon Fowler
Capitol, 1986

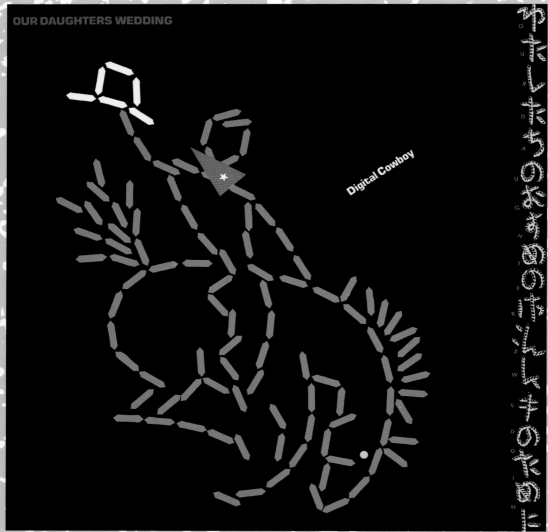

OUR DAUGHTERS WEDDING

Digital Cowboy

Digital Cowboy
OUR DAUGHTERS WEDDING
Cover art: Unknown
EMI America, 1981

The cover for Digital Cowboy explores the realm of digital art, as did the band's music.

ODW

145

ST-17075

OUR DAUGHTERS WEDDING

Moving Windows
OUR DAUGHTERS WEDDING
Cover art: Claire Taylor
Photography: Anders Nordstrom
EMI America, 1982

English Boys/Working Girls
DEAF SCHOOL
Cover art: Kevin Ward
Photography: David Anthony
Warner Bros., 1978

Love Life
BERLIN
Cover art: Richard Seireeni
Photography: Phillip Dixon
Geffen, 1984

TRUE CONFESSIONS
Cover art: Rodney Bowes/Kim Crowder
Photography: Rodney Bowes
Bomb, 1980

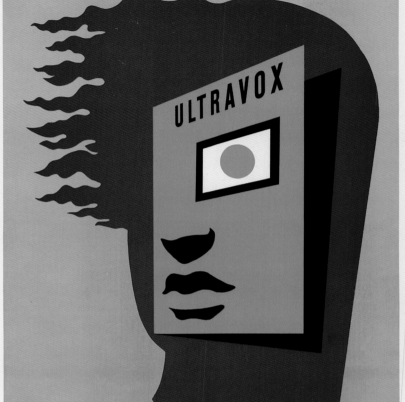

Peter Saville designed this cover for Ultravox as well as Hymn and Quartet.

Rage in Eden
ULTRAVOX
Cover art: Peter Saville
Chrysalis, 1981

the church

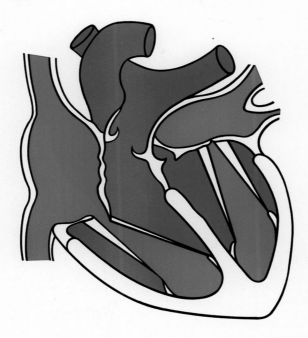

# of skins and heart

Of Skins and Heart
THE CHURCH
Cover art: Steve Kilbey/Michele Parker
Arista, 1981

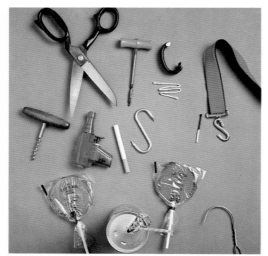

This Is Pop? (Single)
XTC
Cover art: Unknown
Virgin, 1978

Making Plans for Nigel (Single)
XTC
Cover art: Cooke Key/Steve Shotter
Virgin, 1979

XTC's Making Plans for Nigel single included a board game. Many of their singles are collectible, including the 1977 unreleased picture sleeve version of Science Friction ($1500).

Andy Partridge, XTC's guitarist and vocalist, shared credit for the Drums and Wires *cover art, which borrows from the "face" logo design of the 1940s and 1950s.*

Drums and Wires
XTC
Cover art: Andy Partridge/Jill Mumford
Virgin, 1979

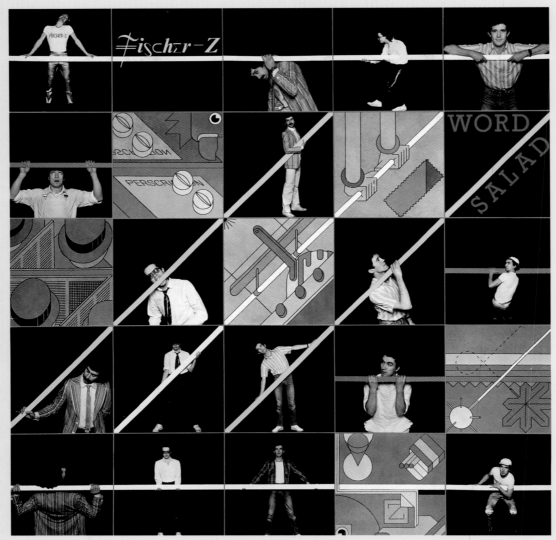

152

Word Salad
FISCHER-Z
Cover art: John Pasche/George Hardie
Photography: James Wedge
United Artists, 1979

Fischer-Z is pronounced the British way [zed] to sound like "fish's head."

=Split= ≤Enz=

D I Z R Y T H M I A

D I Z R Y T H M I A

153

Drummer, vocalist, Noel Crombie, had a hand in the design of several Split Enz covers.

Dizrythmia
SPLIT ENZ
Cover art: Noel Crombie/Peter Wagg
Photography: Han Chew Tham
Mushroom, 1979

ALSO FEATURES THE SMASH SINGLES `I GOT THE MESSAGE´ `ANTARCTICA´

MEN WITHOUT HATS

THE SAFETY DANCE

EXTENDED`CLUB MIX´

154

The Safety Dance
MEN WITHOUT HATS
Cover art: B. WEAR
Statik, 1982

Originally cover art for 12-inch singles was simply enlarged versions of the covers for the 7-inch single, or had no design at all. By the early 1980s the majority featured unique designs.

155

BSR-39002

Rhythm of Youth
MEN WITHOUT HATS
Cover art: Unknown
Backstreet, 1983

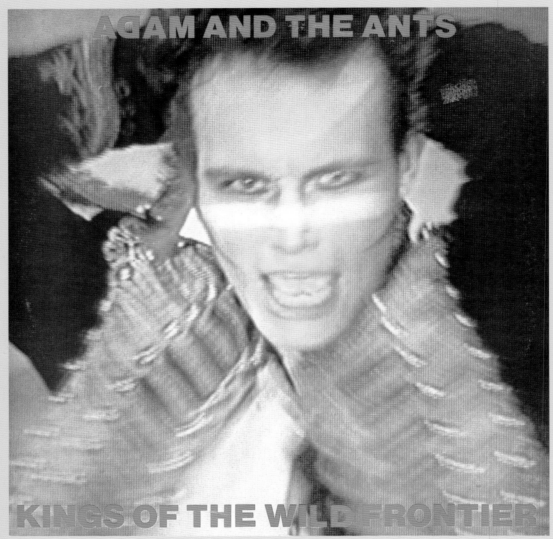

156

ADAM AND THE ANTS

KINGS OF THE WILD FRONTIER

Kings of the Wild Frontier
ADAM AND THE ANTS
Cover art: Adam Ant/Jules
Photography: Peter Ashworth
Epic/CBS, 1980

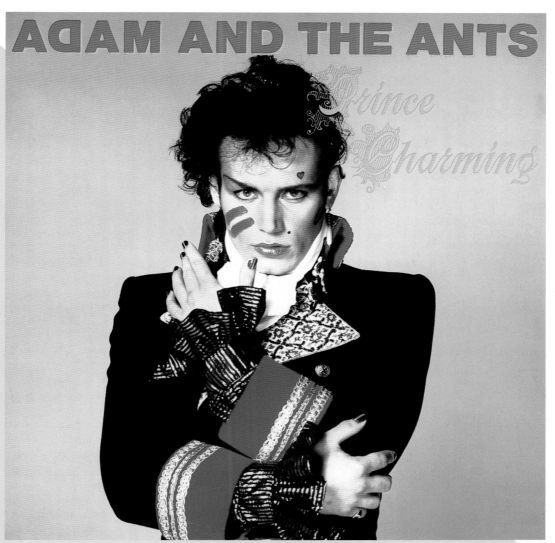

ADAM AND THE ANTS

Adam Ant embodied the New Romantic look.

Prince Charming
ADAM AND THE ANTS
Cover art: Adam Ant/Jules
Photography: Allan Ballard
Epic/CBS, 1981

158

Side Kicks
THOMPSON TWINS
Cover art: Satori/Jeremy Pemberton/David Shortt
Photography: Roger Charity
Arista, 1983

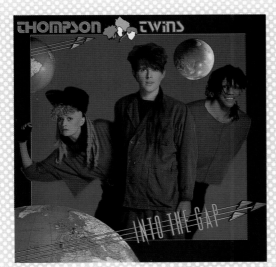

Into the Gap
THOMPSON TWINS
Cover art: Satori/Alannah/Nick Marchant
Photography: Peter Ashworth
Arista, 1984

Suburban Voodoo
PAUL CARRACK
Cover art: Unknown
Photography: Brian Griffin
Epic/CBS, 1982

160

Non-Stop Erotic Cabaret
SOFT CELL
Cover art: Peter Ashworth
Some Bizzare/Sire, 1981

DLP-15001 MINI LP/4 SONGS

MISSING
PERSONS

161

MISSING PERSONS
Cover art: Missing Persons
Photography: Carla Weber
Capitol, 1982

DEBBIE HARRY
Koo Koo

162

KooKoo's giant acupuncture needles correspond to the four elements: eyes (fire), nose (air), mouth (water), and neck (earth).

KooKoo
DEBBIE HARRY
Cover art: H.R. Giger/Peter Wagg
Photography: Brian Aris
Chrysalis, 1981

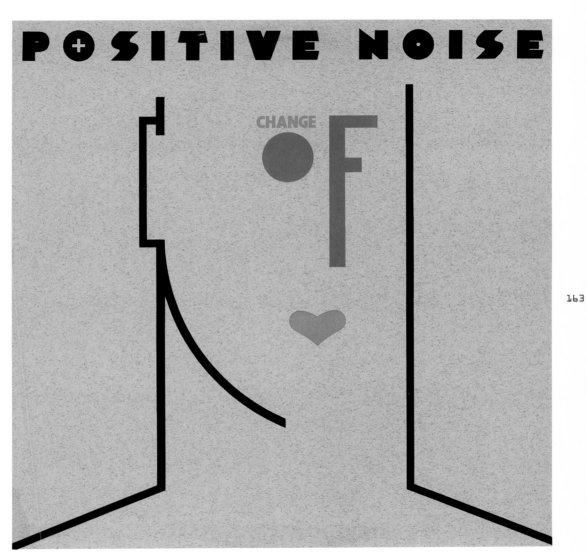

163

Change of Heart
POSITIVE NOISE
Cover art: Unknown
Statik/Sire, 1982

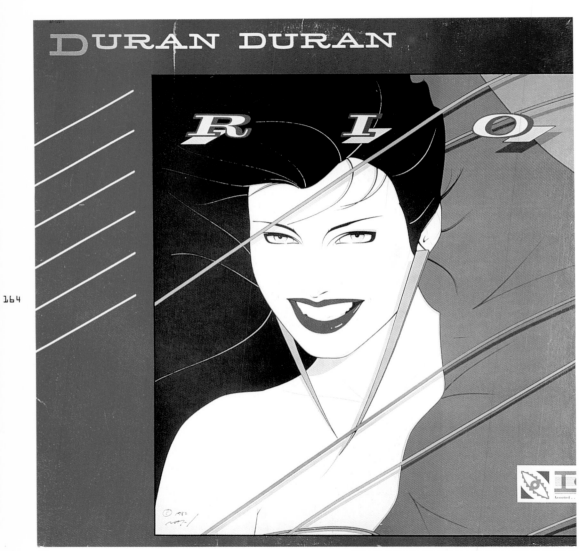

164

Rio
DURAN DURAN
Cover art: Assorted Images/Patrick Nagel
Harvest/EMI, 1982

*Patrick Nagel created graphics editions and posters, as well as illustrations for
Playboy. The "Nagel Woman" with her stark simplicity and elegance became
instantly recognizable and was tremendously popular. Nagel's mass-produced
posters were a fixture in poster shops throughout the 1980s.*

165

Seven and the Ragged Tiger
DURAN DURAN
Cover art: Malcolm Garrett/Keith Breeden/Assorted Images
Capitol, 1983

BRONSKI BEAT

THE AGE OF CONSENT

166

MCA-5538

BRONSKI BEAT

The Age of Consent
BRONSKI BEAT
Cover art: Green Ink
London/MCA, 1984

Hundreds & Thousands
BRONSKI BEAT
Cover art: Green Ink/Jane Suchodolski
Photography: Vantage
London/MCA, 1985

SIMPLE MINDS

SONS AND FASCINATION

Sons and Fascination
SIMPLE MINDS
Cover art: Malcolm Garrett/Assorted Images
Photography: Sheila Rock
Virgin, 1981

SKĀFISH
conversation

Conversation
SKAFISH
Cover art: Glinda Harrison/Dan Winner/Carl Grasso
Photography: Paul Natkin/Photo Reserve
I.R.S., 1983

VISAGE
Cover art: Iain Gillies/Visage/Kate Wilson
Photography: Peter Ashworth/Robyn Beeche
Polydor, 1980

After the Snow
MODERN ENGLISH
Cover art: Vaughan Oliver/23 Envelope
Sire/4 AD, 1982

Visage included Steve Strange, Ultravox's Midge Ure and Billy Currie, as well as
Magazine's Dave Formula.

Echo & The Bunnymen

OCEAN RAIN

For Echo & the Bunnymen's first album, Crocodiles, Griffin photographed the band at night in the woods. For their third, Porcupine, they were photographed at a waterfall in Iceland. The cover for Ocean Rain features the band in a cave.

Ocean Rain
ECHO & THE BUNNYMEN
Cover art: Martyn Atkins
Photography: Brian Griffin
Korova/Sire, 1984

172

Life in a Day
SIMPLE MINDS
Cover art: Carole Moss
Zoom, 1979

Sparkle in the Rain
SIMPLE MINDS
Cover art: Assorted Images
A&M, 1984

MARTHA AND THE MUFFINS

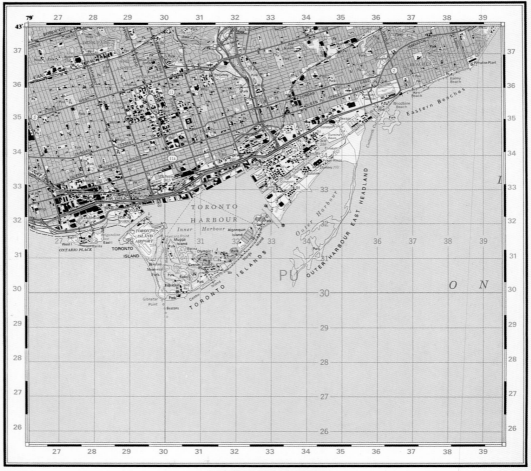

METRO MUSIC

174

Metro Music
MARTHA AND THE MUFFINS
Cover art: Martha and the Muffins/Peter Saville
DinDisc, 1980

Magnets
THE VAPORS
Cover art: John Pasche/Martin Handford
Liberty, 1981

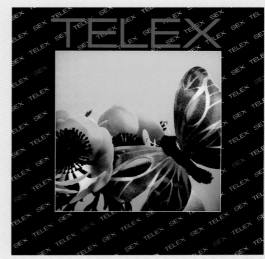

Sex
TELEX
Cover art: Telex
PVC, 1981

The cover illustration on Magnets *is by Martin Handford, creator of the popular*
"Where's Waldo" series.

Straight Lines
NEW MUSIK
Cover art: Paula Scher
GTO/Epic, 1979

Fizz! Pop! (Modern Rock)
THE CONTINENTALS
Cover art: Paula Scher
Epic, 1979

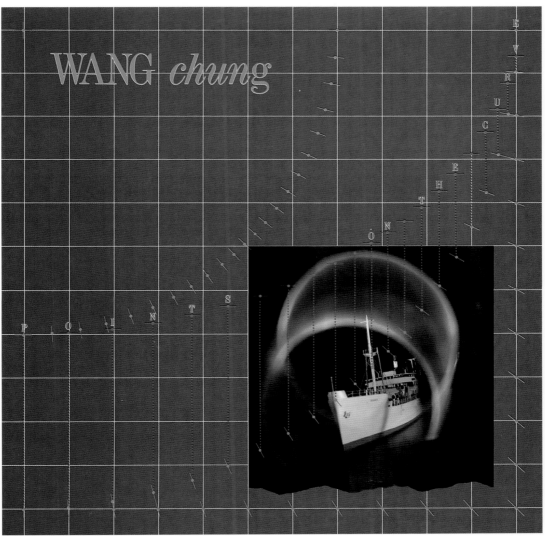

WANG *chung*

EVERY

UCE

HT

ON

POINTS

Barney Bubbles (born Colin Fulcher) was a London-based designer influenced by
Russian Constructivism and Futurism. He designed many covers for New Wave,
including Elvis Costello's Imperial Bedroom and this one for Wang Chung.
Diagnosed with schizophrenia, he committed suicide in 1983.

Points on the Curve
WANG CHUNG
Cover art: Barney Bubbles
Photography: Brian Griffin
Geffen, 1983

THE MOTELS
Cover art: Roy Kohara/Henry Marquez
Photography: Elliot Gilbert
Capitol, 1979

Roy Kohara, the art director at Capitol in the 1980s, won a grammy for best album package for Bob Seger and the Silver Bullet Band's Against the Wind.

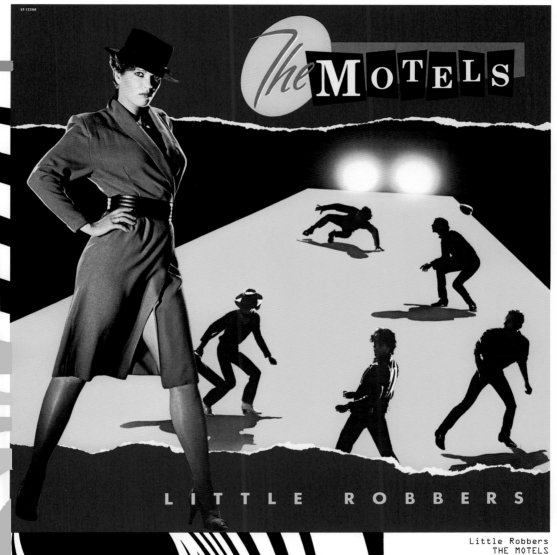

ST-12288

The MOTELS

LITTLE ROBBERS

Little Robbers
THE MOTELS
Cover art: Kosh/Ron Larson
Photography: Bob Blakeman
Capitol, 1983

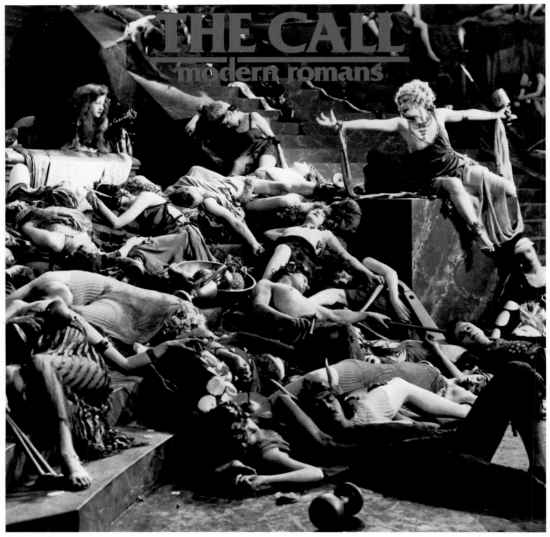

Modern Romans
THE CALL
Cover art: Michael Been/L&W Design
Photography: Paramount Pictures
Mercury/Polygram, 1983

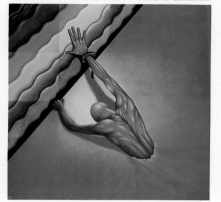

Reach the Beach
THE FIXX
Cover art: George Underwood/Cream
MCA, 1983

Cupid & Psyche
SCRITTI POLITTI
Cover art: Keith Breeden/Green
Virgin/Warner Bros., 1985

Cupid & Psyche *explored digital technology, while cover designer Keith Breeden, along
with singer Green, created a cover that combines the look of glossy advertising with
various textures and unconventional materials such as beeswax and copper.*

ROXY MUSIC
FLESH+BLOOD

182

Flesh+Blood
ROXY MUSIC
Cover art: Bryan Ferry/Antony Price/Neil Kirk/Simon Puxley/Peter Saville
Photography: Neil Kirk
Atco, 1980

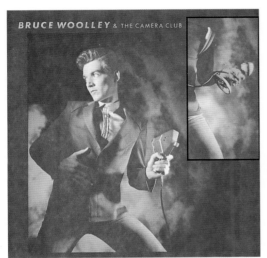

BRUCE WOOLLEY & THE CAMERA CLUB
Cover art: Janet Perr
Photography: Andrew Douglas
Columbia, 1979

Einzelhaft
FALCO
Cover art: Stefan Weber
Photography: Hannes Leipold
A&M, 1982

Bruce Woolley, a former Buggle, co-wrote "Video Killed the Radio Star."

THE HUMAN
LEAGUE
DARE

Dare
THE HUMAN LEAGUE
Cover art: Human League
Photography: Brian Aris
A&M, 1981

The Human League was one of the most successful Synth-Pop bands, hitting it big in the U.S. with "Don't You Want Me." The cover for Dare features a picture lifted from a Vogue magazine cover as well as magazine-style typography.

185

Hysteria
THE HUMAN LEAGUE
Cover art: Ken Ansell
Virgin, 1984

After Eight
TACO
Cover art: Unknown
Photography: Gesine Petter
RCA, 1982

TACO had a big MTV hit with the song "Puttin' on the Ritz."

Feeling Cavalier
EBN OZN
Cover art: Lynn Dreese Breslin
Photography: Virginia Liberatore
Elektra/Asylum, 1984

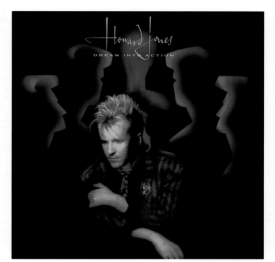

Dream Into Action
HOWARD JONES
Cover art: Rob O'Connor
Photography: Simon Fowler
WEA/Elektra, 1985

Spandau Ballet

True

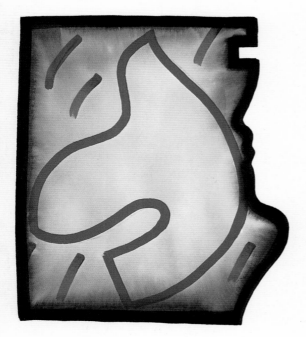

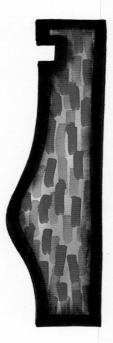

True
SPANDAU BALLET
Cover art: David Band
Chrysalis, 1983

Spandau Ballet, who took their name from graffiti seen in West Berlin, was one of the most popular New Ro bands.

189

White Feathers
KAJAGOOGOO
Cover art: Shoot That Tiger!
Photography: Ian Hooton
EMI America, 1983

NOVEMBER GROUP

NOVEMBER GROUP
Cover art: Ann Prim
Photography: Ann Prim
Modern Method, 1982

HEAVEN 17
SHEFFIELD • EDINBURGH • LONDON
THE LUXURY GAP

Heaven 17's Martyn Ware and Ian Craig Marsh were members of The Human
League until 1980. Along with singer Glenn Gregory, they were also members of
British Electric Foundation.

The Luxury Gap
HEAVEN 17
Cover art: Ray Smith
Virgin/Arista, 1983

192

TINY DESK UNIT
Cover art: Unknown
9¹/₂ X 16, 1980

Claro Que Si
YELLO
Cover art: Unknown
Yello Sound Production/Ralph, 1981

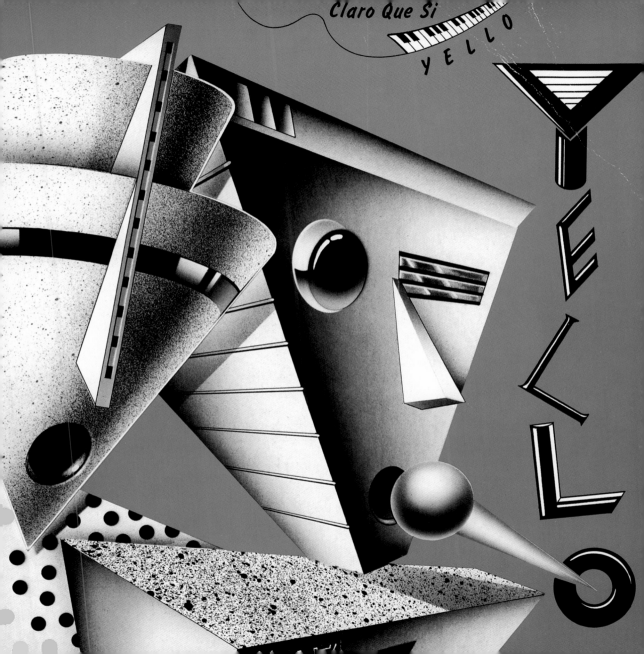

194

(everywhere at once)

Everywhere at Once
THE PLIMSOULS
Cover art: Unknown
Geffen, 1983

MIDGE**U**RE

195

THE**G**IFT

© 1985

The Gift
MIDGE URE
Cover art: Unknown
Chrysalis, 1985

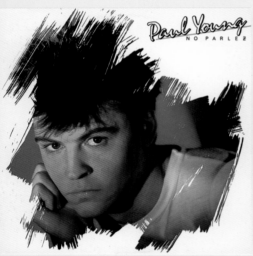

No Parlez
PAUL YOUNG
Cover art: Peter Andrew Alfieri
Photography: Simon Fowler
Columbia, 1983

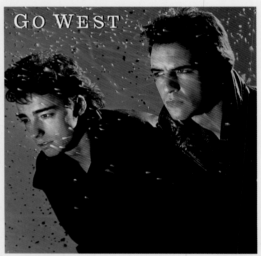

GO WEST
Cover art: John Pasche
Photography: Brian Griffin
Chrysalis, 1985

ICEHOUSE
measure for measure

197

Australian band Icehouse began as Flowers. The band was renamed after the title of the Flowers' LP Icehouse.

Measure for Measure
ICEHOUSE
Cover art: Norman Moore/Rick Dobbis
Photography: Simon Fowler
Chrysalis, 1986

True Colours
SPLIT ENZ
Cover art: Noel Crombie
Mushroom/A&M, 1980

True Colours
SPLIT ENZ
Cover art: Noel Crombie
Mushroom/A&M, 1980

*Three versions of Colours were printed with the same cover design but different
color combinations: red and green, purple and yellow, and blue and orange.*

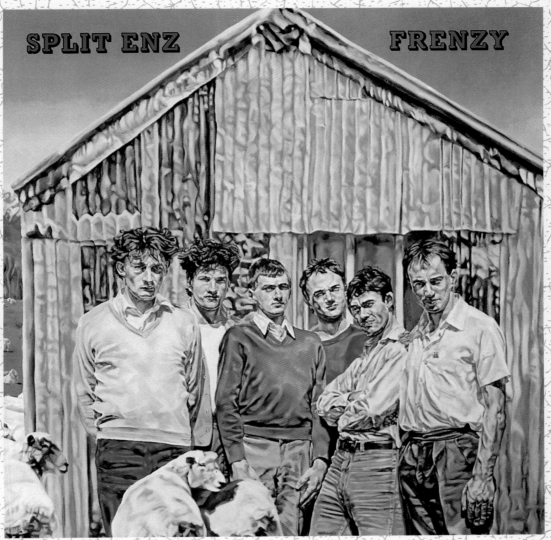

SPLIT ENZ

FRENZY

199

New Zealand artist Raewyn Turner painted the cover of Frenzy. She also designed
the lighting for Split Enz concerts.

Frenzy
SPLIT ENZ
Cover art: Raewyn Turner
Australia-Mushroom/A&M, 1981

Waiata
SPLIT ENZ
Cover art: Unknown
A&M, 1981

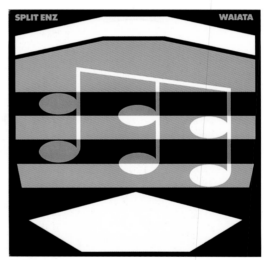

Waiata
SPLIT ENZ
Cover art: Unknown
A&M, 1981

Waiata is the Maori word for party. Following in the trend of True Colours, *A&M issued three different colored covers. The original Australian release was titled* Corroboree.

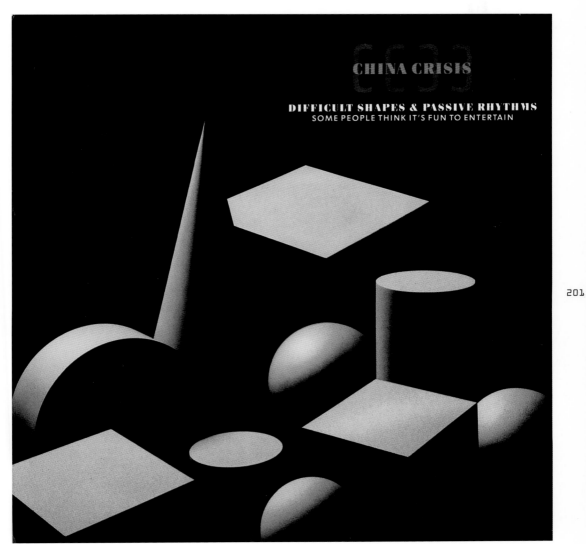

201

Difficult Shapes & Passive Rhythms
CHINA CRISIS
Cover art: Peter Saville Associates
Photography: Trevor Key
Virgin, 1982

LENE LOVICH
(Lāy-nă Lŭv-ĭtch)

STATELESS
(Stāy-t-lĕss)

202

Stateless
LENE LOVICH
Cover art: Chris Morton
Photography: Brian Griffin
Stiff/Epic, 1979

RACHEL SWEET   PROTECT THE INNOCENT

Brian Griffin, who photographed Rachel Sweet for Protect the Innocent, *is best known for his image of Joe Jackson's shoes on* Look Sharp!

Protect the Innocent
RACHEL SWEET
Cover art: Unknown
Photography: Brian Griffin
Stiff/Columbia, 1980

Girls' Night Out
KAREN LAWRENCE & THE PINZ
Cover art: Ron Kellum/Karen Lawrence/Fred Hostetler
Photography: Nick Sangiamo
RCA, 1981

CATHOLIC GIRLS
Cover art: Kathe Schreyer/George Osaki
Photography: Aaron Rapoport
MCA, 1982

10¢ A Dance
THE FLIRTS
Cover art: J. Romero/R. Rovira/Periscope Studio
O-Vanguard, 1982

GO·GO'S

beau
a
t
be

GO·GO'S

207

Vacation

Beauty and the Beat
GO-GO'S
Cover art: Mike Doud/Ginger Canzoneri/Cindy Marsh/Mike Fink
I.R.S., 1981

Vacation
GO-GO'S
Cover art: Mick Haggerty/Ginger Canzoneri
Photography: Mick Haggerty
I.R.S., 1982

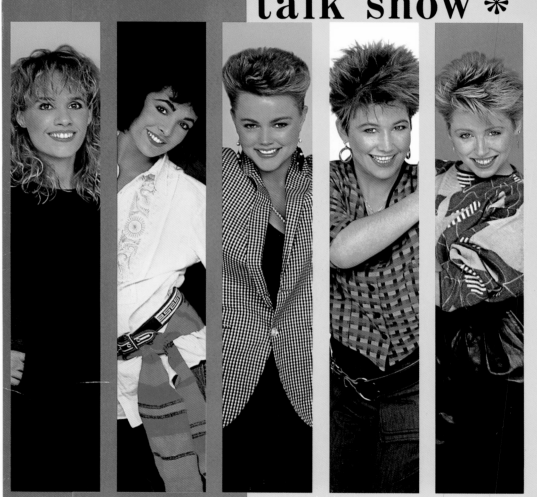

talk show *

Talk Show
GO-GO'S
Cover art: Douglas Brian Martin
Photography: Chris Craymer
I.R.S./A&M, 1984

Parallel Lines
BLONDIE
Cover art: Ramey Communications/Frank Duarte/
Jerry Rodriguez
Photography: Edo
Chrysalis, 1978

Breaking Glass
HAZEL O'CONNOR
Cover art: Chuck Beeson
A&M, 1980

BLUE ANGEL
Cover art: Bob Heimall/Stephanie Zuras
Photography: Benno Friedman
Polydor, 1980

Blue Angel included the soon-to-be-solo singer Cyndi Lauper.

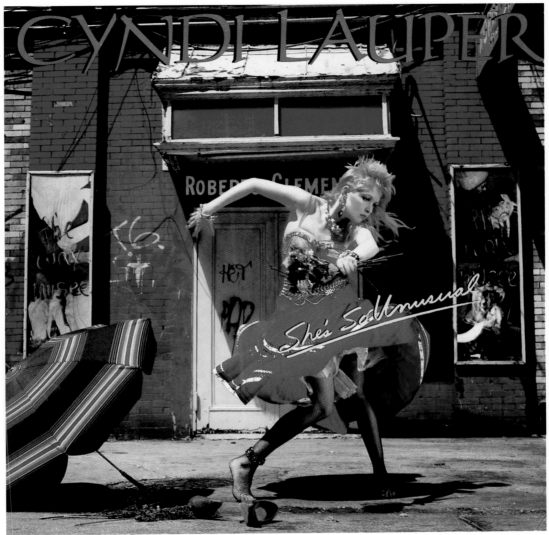

CYNDI LAUPER

Annie Leibovitz shot the cover photograph for She's So Unusual, as well as album covers for Bruce Springsteen, Patti Smith, and Tom Waits.

She's So Unusual
CYNDI LAUPER
Cover art: Cyndi Lauper/Janet Perr
Photography: Annie Leibovitz
Portrait/CBS, 1983

212

NINA HAGEN BAND
Cover art: Unknown
Photography: Jim Rakete
CBS, 1978

NINA HAGEN BAND
Cover art: Gene Greif
Photography: Alain Bizos
CBS, 1978

Translucence
POLY STYRENE
Cover art: Cooke Key
Photography: Falcon Stuart
United Artists, 1980

Poly Styrene was the singer for X-Ray Spex. After the release of Translucence, *she left music to join a religious cult.*

JANE AIRE
AND THE BELVEDERES

JANE AIRE AND THE BELVEDERES
Cover art: Jill Mumford
Photography: Paddy Eckersley
Virgin, 1979

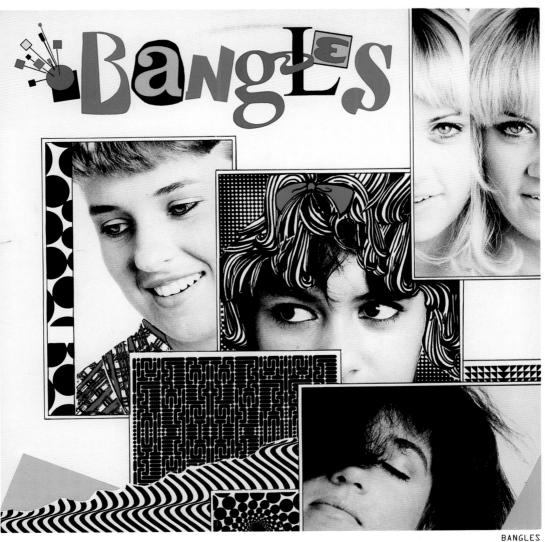

BANGLES
Cover art: Ewa Wojciak
Photography: Bob Seideman
Faulty Products, 1982

In the City
THE JAM
Cover art: Bill Smith/Wadewood Associates
Photography: Martin Goddard
Polydor, 1977

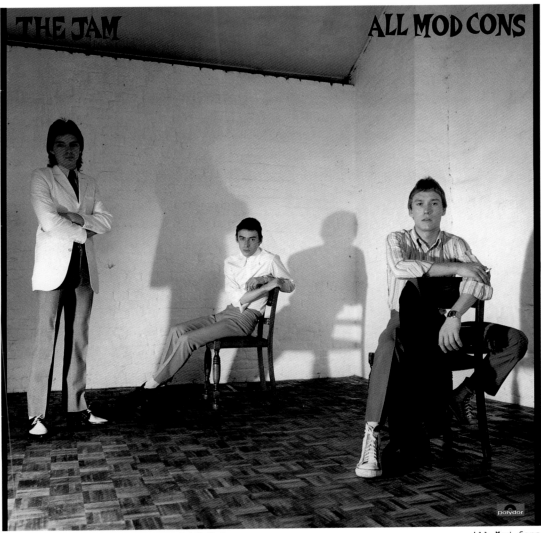

THE JAM

ALL MOD CONS

217

Unlike the New Romantics' explorations of flamboyance, Neo Mods like The Jam,
exhibited their coolness in the subtle details of their dress.

All Mod Cons
THE JAM
Cover art: The Jam/Bill Smith/Jill Mumford
Photography: Peter Kodick
Polydor, 1978

Short Back n' Sides
IAN HUNTER
Cover art: Goto
Photography: Lynn Goldsmith
Chrysalis, 1981

My Ever Changing Moods
THE STYLE COUNCIL
Cover art: Simon Halfon/Paul Weller
Photography: Peter Anderson
Geffen, 1984

*In 1982 The Jam's frontman Paul Weller and Merton Parkas' keyboardist Mick
Talbot formed The Style Council.*

THE STYLE COUNCIL/INTERNATIONALISTS

219

Internationalists
THE STYLE COUNCIL
Cover art: Simon Halfon/Paul Weller
Photography: Nick Knight
Geffen, 1985

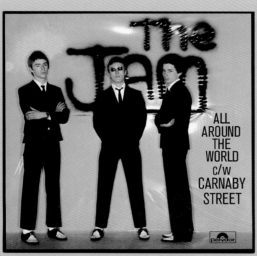

All Around the World (Single)
THE JAM
Cover art: Bill Smith
Photography: Martyn Goddard
Polydor, 1977

Behind Closed Doors
SECRET AFFAIR
Cover art: Keith Breeden
Photography: Andrew Douglas
Arista, 1980

BEAT BOYS IN THE JET AGE ➔ *the LAMBRETTAS*

221

PIG-3257

Beat Boys in the Jet Age
THE LAMBRETTAS
Cover art: Peter Hill/Jubilee Graphics
Photography: Martyn Goddard
The Rocket Record Company/MCA, 1980

I JUST CAN'T STOP IT THE ENGLISH BEAT

222

I Just Can't Stop It
THE ENGLISH BEAT
Cover art: Hunt Emerson/David Shortt
Sire/Go-Feet, 1980

UB40

UNEMPLOYMENT BENEFIT ATTENDANCE CARD

Surname (block capitals)	Initials	NI Number	CODOT No.
M			

Post Office

1 **IMPORTANT NOTICE ABOUT CLAIMING BENEFIT**

MON	
TUES	
WEDS	
THU	
FRI	

Signing box

You should make your claims for unemployment benefit at the Benefit Office each week on the days and at the times shown in the box on the right. Produce this card on each occasion.

If you fail to claim in any week on the day specified you risk losing benefit and you could be disqualified for all the days between your last claim and the day you next claim.

If you do miss claiming benefit on the day specified go to the Benefit Office on the very next day you can (but not on Saturday or Sunday). Do not wait until the specified day in the following week.

This notice ceases to apply when you start work or claim another benefit. If you again become unemployed you should claim benefit on the first day of unemployment.

Surname	Initials	NI Number	chkd by & date

2 **CLAIM FOR OUTSTANDING BENEFIT**

If there is outstanding benefit in respect of days for which you have already claimed, payment will be made by post to your home address **on return of this card with part 3 completed.** If there are days between the last day on which you claimed benefit at the Benefit Office and the date on which you started work (or claimed another benefit) **complete the declaration below:-**

"I HAVE READ AND UNDERSTAND the leaflet 'Responsibility of Claimants' (LB 18).

I CLAIM BENEFIT for the following dates ....

AND DECLARE that on those days I was unemployed and did no work: I was able and willing to do any suitable work but was unable to get any: the circumstances of my dependants were as last stated." **(If there was a change cross out this last item).**

Signature.. date.................

DO NOT SIGN UNTIL THE LAST DAY FOR WHICH YOU WISH TO CLAIM BENEFIT.

SIGNING OFF

223

UB40's first album, Signing Off, *celebrated the fact that some members of the band had "signed off" from the Dole. The album cover depicts an actual Dole Card, "UNEMPLOYMENT BENEFIT 40" or "UB40."*

Signing Off
UB40
Cover art: Geoffrey/David Tristram/UB40
Graduate, 1980

224

WHA'PPEN?

Wha'ppen?
THE ENGLISH BEAT
Cover art: Hunt Emerson/English Beat
Sire/Go-Feet, 1981

Special Beat Service
THE ENGLISH BEAT
Cover art: Martyn Atkins
Photography: Bruce Fleming
I.R.S., 1982

Labour of Love
UB40
Cover art: Kenneth Ansell/David Dragon
Virgin/A&M, 1983

MADNESS

ONE STEP BEYOND...

MADNESS

Keep Moving

One Step Beyond...
MADNESS
Cover art: Eddie and Jules
Photography: Cameron McVey
Sire, 1978

Keep Moving
MADNESS
Cover art: Stiff Art
Photography: Tony Duffy
Geffen, 1984

THE SPECIALS

THE SPECIALS
Cover art: Chalkie Davis/Carol Starr
2-Tone/Chrysalis, 1980

Jerry Dammers of The Specials formed his own label, 2-Tone, helping to revive Ska. The company went on to merge with Chrysalis. 2-Tone's black and white checkered graphics became synonymous with ska. "Walt Jabsco," the hip black and white figure featured on the records and some album covers became a music icon, appearing on badges, T-shirts, and other merchandise. Dammers based Jabsco on a picture of Peter Tosh from The Wailing Wailers *album.*

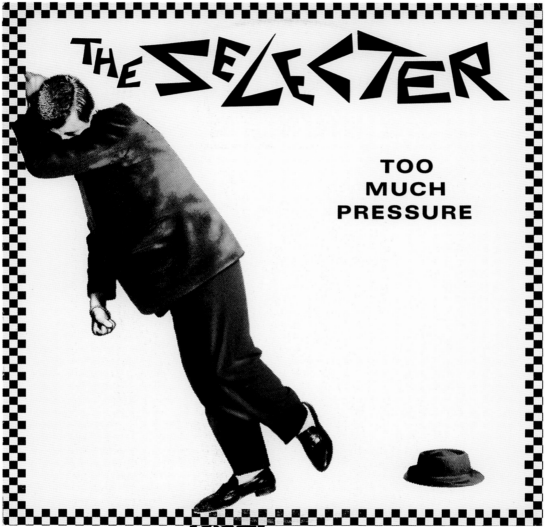

229

Too Much Pressure
THE SELECTER
Cover art: Teflon Sims/David Storey
Photography: Rick Mann
2-Tone/Chrysalis, 1980

THE FUN BOY THREE

FB3

THE FUN BOY THREE
Cover art: John Teflon Sims/Terry Day
Photography: Allan Ballard
Chrysalis, 1982

Waiting
THE FUN BOY THREE
Cover art: David Storey/F.B.3
Photography: Mike Owen
Chrysalis, 1983

230

FUN BOY THREE
WAITING

THE KINGBEES
Cover art: Unknown
RSO/Bronze, 1980

Make a Circuit with Me
POLECATS
Cover art: Polecats/Rockin' Russian
Photography: Sheila Rock/Chris Gabrin
PolyGram, 1983

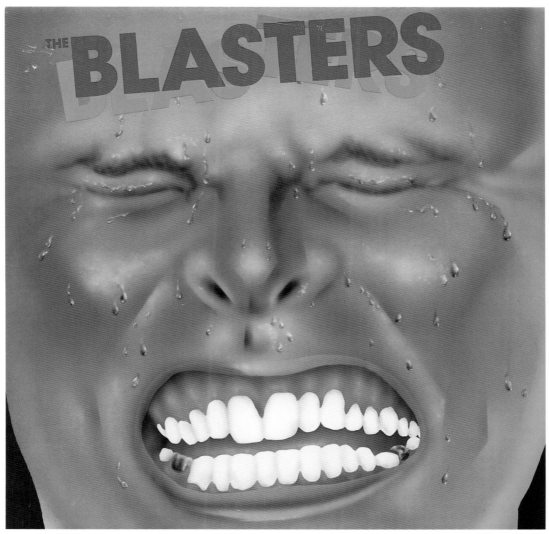

233

THE BLASTERS
Cover art: Gustav Alsina/Steve Bartel
Slash-Warner Bros./F-Beat, 1981

234

Roping Wild Bears
RAYBEATS
Cover art: Trace Rosel/Lisa Rosel
Don't Fall Off the Mountain, 1981

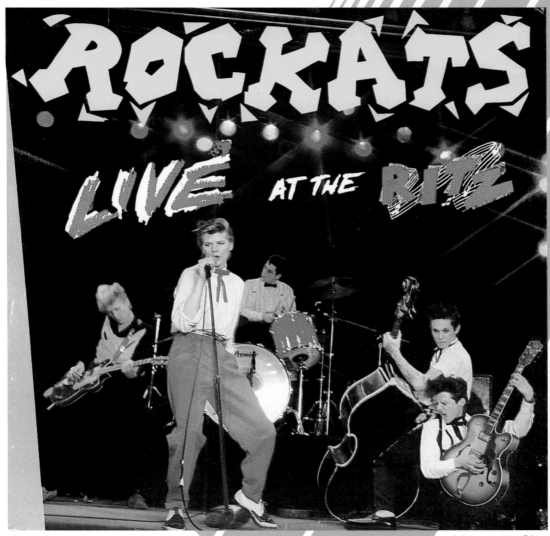

235

Live at the Ritz
ROCKATS
Cover art: Mary Anne Fike/Mick Rock/Rockats
Photography: Mick Rock
Island, 1981

ROBERT GORDON

BAD BOY

236

AFL1-3523 STEREO

Bad Boy
ROBERT GORDON
Cover art: J.J. Stelmach
Photography: Marcia Resnick
RCA, 1980

Rock Billy Boogie
ROBERT GORDON
Cover art: Unknown
RCA, 1979

Are You Gonna Be the One
ROBERT GORDON
Cover art: Robert Gordon/J.J. Stelmach
Photography: Mick Rock
RCA, 1981

Before Robert Gordon became a '50s rocker, he was a member of the Punk band Tuff Darts.

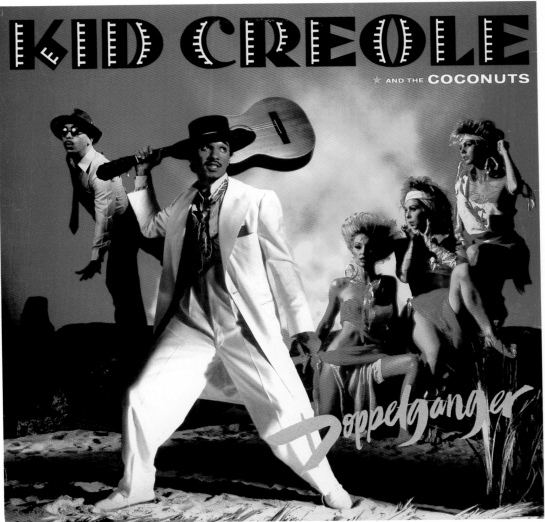

239

DEFUNKT
Cover art: M & Co.
Hannibal, 1980

Doppelganger
KID CREOLE AND THE COCONUTS
Cover art: Bruno Tilley
Photography: Peter Ashworth
ZE/Sire, 1983

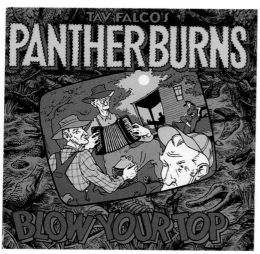

Blow Your Top
TAV FALCO'S PANTHER BURNS
Cover art: Michael McMahon
Photography: Julienne Schaer
Animal, 1982

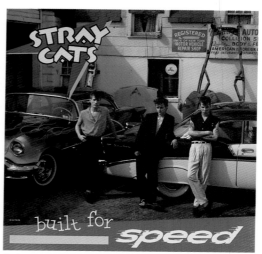

Built for Speed
STRAY CATS
Cover art: Charles Novick Studios/Francesca
Photography: Gavin Cochrane
EMI America, 1982

Rant n' Rave with the Stray Cats
STRAY CATS
Cover art: Henry Marquez
Photography: Gavin Cochrane
EMI America, 1983

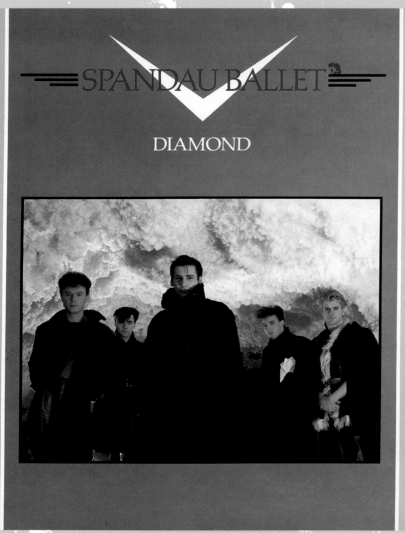

242

Diamond
SPANDAU BALLET
Cover art: Graham Smith
Photography: Andy Earl
Chrysalis, 1982

Spoons

243

Arias & Symphonies

Arias & Symphonies
SPOONS
Cover art: M.P. Krawczynski/P.L. Noble/Gordon Deppe
A&M, 1982

LANDSCAPE

From the Tea-rooms of Mars ....

From the Tea-rooms of Mars ....
LANDSCAPE
Cover art: Andrew Christian/John Warwicker
Photography: Ray Massey
RCA, 1981

Landscape was led by Richard Burgess, producer of Spandau Ballet and Visage.

DEPECHE MODE
A BROKEN FRAME

Rollingstone *chose Town and Country Planning's socialist-themed cover for* A
Broken Frame *as one of the 100 best album covers.*

A Broken Frame
DEPECHE MODE
Cover art: Martyn Atkins/Town and Country Planning
Photography: Brian Griffin
Sire/Mute, 1982

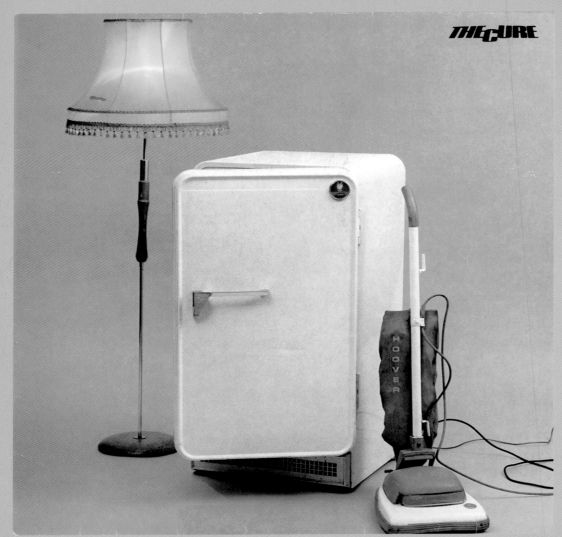

THE CURE

246

Three Imaginary Boys
THE CURE
Cover art: Bill Smith
Photography: Martyn Goddard
Fiction, 1979

BOYS DON'T CRY THE CURE

247

Boys Don't Cry
THE CURE
Cover art: Bill Smith
PVC, 1980

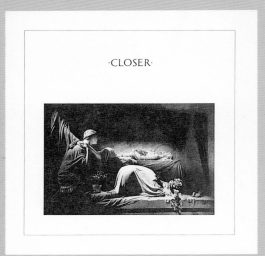

Closer
JOY DIVISION
Cover art: Peter Saville/Martyn Atkins
Photography: Bernard Pierre Wolff
Factory, 1980

CLASSIX NOUVEAUX
Cover art: John Pasche
Photography: Jay Myrdal
Liberty United, 1980

Joy Division's lead singer, Ian Curtis, killed himself in 1981, shortly after Closer, a somber album. The album cover, designed by Martyn Atkins and Peter Saville, features a photograph of an Italian funeral statuary by French photographer Bernard Pierre Wolff.

BAUHAUS

The cover illustration for Mask is by Daniel Ash, Bauhaus guitarist and vocalist. Ash attended art school before forming Bauhaus with childhood friend Peter Murphy. After Bauhaus, he went on to form the bands Tones on Tail and Love and Rockets.

Mask
BAUHAUS
Cover art: Daniel Ash
Beggars Banquet, 1981

Playground Twist (Single)
SIOUXSIE AND THE BANSHEES
Cover art: Unknown
Polydor, 1979

Christine (Single)
SIOUXSIE AND THE BANSHEES
Cover art: Rob O'Connor
Photography: Paddy Eckersley
Polydor, 1980

The cover for Hai!, a live recording of a 1982 Cabaret Voltaire concert in Japan, combines electronic typography with Japanese imagery. The band explored electronic music, experimenting with found sounds and tape manipulations.

Hai!
CABARET VOLTAIRE
Cover art: G House
Photography: Richard Kirk
Rough Trade, 1982

INDEX

253

BIBLIOGRAPHY

Books

Dean, Roger and David Howells. *Album Cover Album: The Second Volume*. New York: A&W Visual Library, 1982.

Dean, Roger, David Howells, Bob Fisher, and Colin Greenland. *Album Cover Album: Volume III*. New York: St. Martin's Press, 1984.

DeFoe, B. George and Martha. *International Discography of the New Wave*. New York: Omnibus Press/One Ten Records, 1982.

Larkin, Colin. *The Virgin Encyclopedia of Indie & New Wave*. London: Virgin Publishing, 1998.

Ochs, Michael. *1000 Record Covers*. Köln: Taschen, 2000.

Rettenmund, Matthew. *Totally Awesome 80s*. New York: St. Martin's Griffin, 1996.

Rimmer, Dave. *The Look: New Romantics*. London: Omnibus Press, 2003.

Robbins, Ira A. *The Trouser Press Guide to New Wave Records*. New York: Charles Scribner's Sons, 1983.

Shaw, Greg. *New Wave on Record: 1975-1978*. Burbank, CA: Bomp Books, 1978.

Stanley, John. *Miller's Collecting Vinyl*. London: Octopus Publishing Group Ltd., 2002.

Articles

Azerrad, Michael, Steve Futterman, Elysa Gardner, Michael Goldberg, Alan Light, Kara Manning, Chris Mundy, Kim Neely and Parke Puterbaugh. "100 Classic Album Covers." *Rollingstone,* 14 November 1991.

Brophy, Philip. "Post Punk Graphics: The Displaced Present, Perfectly Placed" *Stuffing No.2*. Retrieved June 15, 2004 from Media Arts, on the World Wide Web: *http://media-arts.rmit.edu.au/Phil_Brophy/PostPunkGraphics.html*.

Gamboa, Glenn. "Rock and Roll is Self-Correcting." *Newsday*, 17 March 2002.

Grant, Angelynn. "Album Cover Design." *Communication Arts* (January/February 2001).

Hansen, Beck. "Cover Power." *Vanity Fair* (November 2001): 210-222.

"New Wave." Retrieved April 5, 2004 from Nostalgia Central, on the World Wide Web: *http://www.nostalgiacentral.com/music/newwave.htm*.

Paulsen, Mike. "A Brief History & Reflections on New Wave." Retrieved January 15, 2004 from New Wave Outpost, on the World Wide Web: *http://www.nwoutpost.com*.

Reynolds, Simon. "The 70's Are So 90's. The 80's Are the Thing Now." *The New York Times*, 5 May 2002.

Strauss, Neil. "The Pop Life; Judging Covers As Artworks." *The New York Times,* 7 June 2001.

Urquhart, Sidney. "Rock-'n'-Roll Cover Up." *Time,* 19 August 1991.

Weir, Jason and Peter Walsh. "The 2 Tone Label." Retrieved June 7, 2004 from 2-Tone Info, on the World Wide Web: *http://2-tone.info/*.